LIVING THE V.I.C.T.O.R.Y. MODEL

DO YOU HAVE WHAT IT TAKES?

The Critical Traits of All Successful People

WALTER NUSBAUM

Do You Have What it Takes?
The Critical Traits of All Successful People

Library of Congress Control Number 2015900604
ISBN 978-0-9863236-1-4

Books may be purchased by contacting the publisher and author at:
walter@walternusbaum.com

Printed in the United States of America
First Printing: January 2015

Trademarks

Cover Designer:
Results by Design, LLC
www.rbdbranding.com

Interior Layout and Design:
Sarah E. Mathewson

Copy Editors:
Sarah E. Mathewson
Brian D. Stuart

Comic Artist:
David Wilborn
www.urbanjunglecomic.com

Published by
StoneGate Publishers
2236 Stonegate Drive
Denton, Texas 76205

Library of Congress Control Number 2015900604

ISBN 978-0-9863236-1-4

PRAISE FOR
DO YOU HAVE WHAT IT TAKES?

“The VICTORY model in this book is one of the most effective I’ve seen at improving people’s professional and personal lives. This is a very important book for anyone who takes success seriously.”

- Matt Seward, CEO, Innovative Partners

“Walter is a very gifted and engaging speaker and has a unique ability to communicate, educate and inspire all people. Our team benefits greatly from his work- and now his book.”

- Kenneth Randall, CEO, Artesia General Hospital

“The VICTORY model is dead on when it comes to people succeeding in our organization.”

- Jessica Simer, HR Manager, HollyFrontier Corporation

“This book is not only motivating, it shows you how to get the most out of anything you do.”

- J.L. Jackson, (Former) President of Diamond Shamrock

“Walter has narrowed the critical elements of success into a set of powerful and memorable principles that can improve any area of your life.”

- Dr. Azam Anwar, Cardiologist & Medical Device Entrepreneur

“The workings of our operations team continue to improve thanks to the VICTORY model. I could not be more supportive of the model and the practical benefits it offers toward achieving success.”

- Mark Cunningham, Senior V.P. Operations at Holly Energy Partners

---

“*Do You Have What it Takes?* will not only help advance your business, but it will improve your life!”

- Mike McCullough, Partner at Bruegger & McCullough, P.C.

ACKNOWLEDGMENTS

There are many people who have been critical to my understanding of what true success looks like. The following list, though far from exhaustive, includes some of those I want to thank in particular for their impact on my life over the years:

- My mother, who always believes I have what it takes. Thank you mom for your never-wavering faith in me. I love you.
- My father, whose recent passing has shown me the importance of having a great legacy. I love you dad and dedicate all that I do to your wonderful memory.
- My brother Mark whose influence extends far beyond this world.
- T.N. whose investment in me is still ever present.
- M.W. whose imprint on me will never go away.
- M.S. whose life and friendship could not have come at a better time.
- C.B. whose love and belief in me will never be forgotten.
- D.M. whose demonstration of grace and love inspires me.
- D.C. who has shown that blood isn't the only form of brotherhood.
- R.H. who never gave up on me, for which I will forever be grateful.
- D.C.C. where I learned what it means to have a second family.
- All my clients for all of your friendships and support.
- To Nick, Josh, and Whitney, three gifts that have surpassed what I deserve.
- My son Cooper, the treasure and delight of my life; I love you inexhaustibly.
- My darling wife Stacey who models all that I write in this book; I love you.
- Finally and most importantly, I give all thanks to the Lord for His ever present love and patience in my life. To know I am loved through the best and worst seasons of my life is a comfort that cannot be described in words.

CONTENTS

WHY THIS BOOK?

If you are anything like me, when you grab a book you usually go straight to the first chapter. I mean, why would you want to read the author's introductory thoughts when all of that material is going to be presented later? I've learned to stop doing that because I realized that a good introduction is like a good appetizer: it prepares you for the rest of the book and it should make you look forward to hearing more from the author. By the time you reach the first page of chapter one, my hope is that you will be excited about what's ahead.

I don't want this to be one of those books where you arrive at chapter three, insert a book mark, get distracted and never go back. I have no doubt that if you read through to the end and take what is said seriously, you will see enormous improvements in every important area of your life. I know we live in a day where it's commonplace for people to make big and bold claims just to sell books, but that is not the case with this book. It's a promise I can make based on my own life experience, as well as the lives of countless numbers of successful people I've known and studied over the years. Whether it's your company, your personal relationships, your financial ambitions or your personal faith, you will see drastic improvements in all areas of your life if you understand and implement the principles described in this book. Even if you feel that you are content with where your life is right now, I assure you that when you finish this book, you will have gained a valuable understanding of several core principles and practices that can lead you to even greater satisfaction in your life.

One of the lessons I've learned from the people around me is that being successful at anything is simple -- but it's not easy. Successful plans are rarely complicated, but their execution always takes a lot of dedication. The principles I share in the pages that follow won't be difficult to understand, but they will require persistence. I can virtually guarantee that if you follow these principles closely and complete the exercises at the end of each chapter, you will accomplish things that you hoped for but maybe never imagined possible. I promise.

With so many books on the market that talk about success, you might ask why I would choose to write another one? In fact as I was writing this book, I was asked that specific question multiple times by my friends. What could possibly be different with this book? It's a very good question and one that deserves a good answer. Over the past 75 years there have been some absolutely wonderful books written on the subject of success and achievement. I have gleaned much insight and wisdom through many of these authors and I have used much of their material to help myself and others. With that being said, I also realized after having read so many of these books that very few of them were written in a way that would make the content easy to recall and apply in our day-to-day lives. Like so many books that we have read, after some time goes by, we may remember the gist of the book and maybe even a few of the key points, but our ability to recall the core content of an entire book can be very challenging. So when I first decided to begin writing a book on the subject of achievement, I knew that I had to communicate my core ideas in a memorable and practical way. So as you read through this book you will discover a model that is both easy to remember and highly practical. Let me give you a great example of this. Not long ago, I met with a friend that I hadn't seen in about four months. He asked me how my book was coming along and if I felt good about it. I decided to test how easy it was to remember what my book is about by asking him if he remembered the core model. To my very pleasant surprise, after four months had passed since we went over it, he repeated the model perfectly in about 20 seconds. That's exactly what I was hoping for. This is one of the reasons I wrote it. It's a book that gives you a model that has been proven by countless numbers of people over time and that can be easily applied in any area of your life.

The VICTORY model that you will read about will be locked in your brain and ready for use immediately. Not only that, but because the main points are all universal principles, you will find yourself agreeing with them without any resistance. Therefore, with discipline and practice, applying this book to your life will become second nature. I have taken some classic principles that are essential to every area of success and arranged them in a model that can be applied in any professional or personal setting.

There are certainly many other great resources out there for you to work through and I will highly recommend many of them to you at the end. These other books will help you continue to refine your understanding and pursuit of personal growth and development. But before we consider these other sources of information, I want to urge you to read on. I am confident you will find the model in this book to be extraordinarily helpful. My goal is to help you get where you want to go and I am convinced that this book can be an instrumental tool in your hands to help you get there.

All you need to bring is a desire to focus, a dedication to do the work and a decision to make the most of your time. With these three things and a proven model of success which is laid out in the pages that follow, I assure you that great things are ahead.

One of my favorite poems that inspires me every time I read it is by Henry Van Dyke. It makes me realize how important *now* is because it's the only aspect of time we can control. As you learn more about the VICTORY Model and how to apply it to your life every day, I hope you will be inspired to make the most of your time.

> "The shadow by my finger cast
> Divides the future from the past:
> Before it, sleeps the unborn hour
> In darkness, and beyond thy power:
> Behind its unreturning line,
> The vanished hour, no longer thine:
> One hour alone is in thy hands,--
> The NOW on which the shadow stands."
>
> *- Henry Van Dyke*

NOTE

AUTHOR'S NOTE

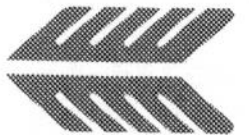

I thought long and hard with my editor about what title and image would best capture the essence of this book. Certainly, it's one of the most critical features of any book. We can believe that a book should not be judged by its cover, but as a point of fact, it almost always is.

One day my very talented editor, Sarah, called and said she had an idea for a title that she believed really captured the essence of what this book is all about. She said, "What if we called it *Do You Have What It Takes?* We could fade out the word *Do* and make the rest of the title *You Have What It Takes* in bold type, illustrating that everyone *has what it takes* ... if they would just tap into what is already within them." She added, "The reason the title is in the form of a question is because most people do not *fully* tap into what they are already *fully* capable of. By reading your book, they can see what those areas are and realize that, in fact, they *do have what it takes!*"

Needless to say, I loved it because it captured exactly what I have observed over many years in the lives of others, as well as through personal experience. I firmly believe that anyone who reads this book absolutely has what it takes to achieve far more than they ever thought possible in every area of their life. There is nothing that I talk about in the following pages that cannot be done by every single person.

I then began to think about what image would best capture the heart of the book. One day I was talking with my good friend, Brad, who also happens to be one of the best skeet shooters in the country, competing on multiple levels including the U.S. Open Skeet Shooting Championship. I love to ask Brad about the mechanics of shooting a moving target and the skills and practices required to be as proficient as he is. It occurred to me that the image for my book had to incorporate the idea of aiming at a target just like Brad does every time he goes out to shoot. That's when the picture of a bull's-eye and an arrow made total sense to me.

The same principles that exist for success in archery also apply to every area of life if you want to be truly successful. Everything from needing to have a clear view of the target, to the necessity of a having a finely-crafted arrow, to the repetitious practice that's required to have great proficiency have parallels in the broader areas of life.

I think most people would be fascinated to watch an arrow fly for a great distance and see it land smack in the middle of a bull's-eye, not just because of the skill that is required, but because there is something about that imagery that speaks to us all. Everyone would love to know they could hit the bull's-eye of success whenever they tried. Whether it's our finances, our relationships, our work life or our spiritual lives, knowing how to hit the bull's-eye consistently would be an enormous satisfaction.

Well that's what this book is all about. It's a book that is simple, practical and very specific about what is required of you. The good news is that all of it is already within your ability. You just have to become more aware of what the key elements of success are and commit yourself to growing and developing in each of these areas. Do this and I promise the arrows of your life will hit far more bull's-eyes than you ever thought possible.

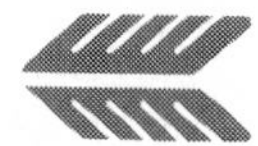

INTRODUCTION

In September of 2011, I was flying to speak to a large business group on the importance of leadership. It was a night flight, which I love, because it allows my mind to relax and reflect. As I sat by the window staring out over the darkness, an idea entered my head (apparently) out of nowhere (you will see later that these types of thoughts NEVER come from nowhere). I grabbed a blank sheet of paper and began writing the names of everyone I personally knew who had achieved significant success in a particular area of their life. Many who made my list had realized great financial success, though this is not why they came to mind. They stood out because of what it took for them to succeed. I then moved to athletes who had achieved significant success in college or at the professional level. These names flowed from my mind easily because their accomplishments stood out above those of their competitors. I then began to think of examples of other categories of successful people. I wrote down the names of married couples who have stayed in love for decades (my parents, for example, who are now on year 47!), mothers and fathers who had extraordinary relationships with their children, musicians and artists who had risen to prominence for their work, and people I knew who had a deep and vibrant spiritual faith. What a list! It was a virtual Who's Who of acquaintances I admire greatly for what they have accomplished in each of those significant areas of their lives. Once I wrote all the names, I began to write beside each name the key traits with which I associated them. At this point I knew I was on to something. What I found particularly fascinating were the common traits that extended across completely different categories. It was as if the very same rules that applied in one area of life also applied in every other area.

As soon as I landed and got to my hotel, I continued the exercise until I had written descriptions and identified traits for every person on the list. Next, I sifted through all the traits and looked for the commonalities. I started creating categories. Seeing mothers and teachers alongside great athletes and brilliant business people all practicing the same core rules of successful living was quite a revelation. The basic principles for being a great parent are EXACTLY the same for being a great CEO. Once all the names and words were scribbled on multiple sheets of paper and categorized, I identified seven basic traits successful people exhibit more effectively than everyone else. The great news about these seven rules is that literally anyone can follow them and enjoy the same results -- if they are willing to put the work in.

Think of the most important areas of your life. Imagine dramatic improvements in all of them. Your business is more productive and fulfilling. Your marriage is deeper and more satisfying. Your relationship with your children is closer. Your department or team is more unified and inspired. Your faith is richer and more alive. All of these things are definitely achievable. Why can't they be? We all have deep longings for things to be better in some facets of life, don't we? I don't know anyone that doesn't want better relationships, greater success at work, and a deeper and more satisfying life. It all comes down to what you are willing to do every day to ensure that when it's all said and done, nothing has been left on the table. You have done everything you can to make the most of everything that is important to you. No regrets. In fact, what's even better is that you leave a legacy that impacts the lives of people all around you long after you are gone. Now that's a life well spent. That's a life of success. That is a life of VICTORY.

THE V.I.C.T.O.R.Y. MODEL

VISION

ZACK, IT'S TIME TO DISCUSS YOUR CAREER GOALS.
©2013 DAVID WILBORN

MY GOAL IS TO SURVIVE THE NEXT THIRTY YEARS AT THIS JOB,
THEN RETIRE A BITTER HUSK OF A MAN WHO'S WASTED HIS WHOLE LIFE IN FRONT OF A COMPUTER SCREEN.

I'LL PUT "MEETING GOALS IN CURRENT POSITION."
GREAT.

"Every man takes the limits of his own field of vision for the limits of the world."

- Arthur Schopenhauer

O N E

THE NECESSITY OF VISION

I can't tell you how many times I have seen people's eyes roll when they hear someone talk about the importance of vision. Most times when I walk into a company that has its vision statement on the wall, employees either don't know what it says, or they know but it doesn't drive their day-to-day decision making. Sadly, the concept of vision has become abstract and uninspiring. Most people see vision as being no different from goals. When you ask someone what their vision is, they often rattle off a list of things they hope to achieve. Granted, goals are related to vision. But goals are not vision. Vision is something much grander, more powerful and more inspiring when understood and effectively pursued.

Not long ago I was leading an all-day off-site exercise for a medical technology company. As we discussed the importance of writing an inspiring vision statement, one of the founding partners blurted, "I don't mean to be rude, but what purpose does this possibly serve?" I loved the honesty of what he said. Unfortunately, his statement reflects the sentiments of many. What skeptics fail to realize is that everyone has to begin with a clear vision. That's the only way to know what steps need to be taken to achieve your ultimate goals. I can understand why this gentleman said what he did. The visioning exercise would only be valuable if the end product was useful. My task, therefore, was more fundamental than simply helping the company craft a strong vision statement. I had to start by helping these executives appreciate the critical importance of clearly defining where they wanted their company to go and what success would ultimately look like for them.

I cannot stress enough how foundational this is. No nation, no military and no organization has ever achieved anything great without the prerequisite of having a clear vision of what they ultimately wanted.

Much wisdom can be found in the biblical Proverb:

> "Where there is no vision, my people perish."
>
> *Proverbs 29:18*

Although this Proverb focuses on God's revelation to man, the general principle can be applied to our daily lives. If people do not have a real vision, many of the possibilities they could have achieved will never materialize. Put simply, you must clearly define what you really want in order to achieve it.

Clarity of Vision

A clear vision is necessary to know what specific actions are required to get you to your desired destination. It's that simple. Most people live their lives reacting to their day-to-day responsibilities. The problem with this approach is obvious. Unless you have a clear picture of what you want, you will go through life bouncing from activity to activity, but you won't be focused on the biggest and most significant areas of your life. What's worse is that you will never get time back. In order to truly achieve great things in your life, whether it's a successful business, an incredible marriage or a healthy lifestyle, you must start with being very clear about what you want the end result to look like.

If you asked highly accomplished people if they clearly knew what they wanted to achieve, the majority would answer with an unequivocal YES. Think of some of the classic examples. I've listed several people below whose lives are characterized by significant achievements. Take a minute and beside each name write what you think they would have said their vision was.

George Washington ______________________________

Abraham Lincoln ______________________________

Henry Ford ______________________________

John Rockefeller ______________________________

Thomas Edison ______________________________

Sam Walton ______________________________

Susan B. Anthony ______________________________

Oprah Winfrey ______________________________

Bill Gates ______________________________

Steve Jobs ______________________________

Mark Zuckerberg ______________________________

Hank Aaron ______________________________

Jackie Robinson ______________________________

Martin Luther King Jr. ______________________________

Albert Einstein ______________________________

Jesus Christ ______________________________

All of these people knew what they wanted to achieve. They were all-consumed by a passion to impact the world in very specific ways. It is important to realize that the majority of these people were ordinary men and women. They faced the same challenges you and I face. What distinguished them was having a clear vision and a determination to make it the fundamental passion driving their life. You and I are no different. We want our lives to count. What most of us lack is the clarity of a compelling vision. You can begin changing that today. It will require some time and self-reflection, but I honestly believe that great visions are inside all of us. There are some great exercises at the end of this chapter that will help you to begin working through the process of finding your compelling vision.

Vision and Passion

Can you think of someone you know whose life's vision is so clear and powerful that it continually shapes their thoughts and actions? Do you know someone whose every choice is designed to get them a step closer to making their vision a reality? I sure can. Her name is Kathy and she is quite a remarkable woman.

I had heard about her for years before we met. People told me what an incredible person she was. Kathy had counseled countless numbers of men and women through some of life's most difficult challenges -- illnesses, addictions, abuse, depression, broken relationships and much more. I heard her name mentioned all the time. I remember hoping that someday I would meet Kathy and see for myself what makes her tick. I learned from those who knew her that she often went out of her way to meet people wherever was most convenient for them. She accompanied her clients to doctor's appointments. She went to divorce hearings and it wasn't unusual for her to drive 20 miles if that made a counseling session more convenient for the client. Talk about dedication and commitment to a passion in life.

Who does that today? I'll tell you who. It's someone who has been captivated by a vision for their life and who feels compelled to do whatever it takes to fulfill that vision.

After several years, I finally had the privilege of getting to know Kathy and learning more about what drives her. She spoke with passion about fulfilling a desire she had possessed for decades. That vision was confirmed by the energy she felt each time she helped someone. Over the years, her vision became a clear, almost tangible, minds-eye view of a project that would represent her life's work. Every person she helped simply added fuel to her fire and brought her one step closer to fulfilling her vision for her life.

Kathy's dream is to build a beautiful in-patient treatment center that offers long-term hope and healing from a Christian perspective to people who are emotionally hurting and desperately need intervention. Listening to Kathy describe the property, the facility and how the center will work would make you think the place had existed for years. What makes Kathy successful is how effectively she integrates her vision into her daily life. In fact, she has thought like a visionary for so long that it takes little effort. It flows naturally out of her because it has been so ingrained in her over many years.

Seeing your life and seeing your purpose in pictures and images is the power behind vision. This is different from wishes or hopes. I would wager that most of us have had moments where we saw a house that seemed ideal and thought, "Wow, I would love something like that!" That may be true, but that is not vision. That is merely a wish. Maybe we start thinking about our health and tell ourselves how much we would love to lose weight. Maybe we see someone playing the piano or the guitar and we tell ourselves how great it would be to learn to play an instrument. Maybe you might even want a promotion at work. No matter what stirs your heart, it has to go beyond just having nice feelings about what you wish would happen. This is NOT what qualifies as a vision.

Having read dozens of definitions of what vision is, allow me to provide my definition. I believe you will find it simple and practical. Vision is:

> "A specific and constantly recurring image that instills passion and drives your commitment to achieve it."

This definition is critical to understand if you want to reap the benefits. So, let's take a moment and break this definition down.

Vision is Specific

First of all, vision is "specific." When you see an image in your mind that is connected to your vision, it will be filled with vivid detail and specific qualities you long to see materialize. Remember Kathy's vision of the in-patient treatment center? She had a mental picture of a center in a country setting surrounded by open land. She envisioned exactly what the building will look like. She had very clear images of the landscape and what it will feel like to drive up to the center for the first time. She could picture the rooms, the offices, the lobby and all the other amenities. At the same time, her heart is filled with emotion as she pictures the center's construction from the ground up. This is one of the critical differences between a vision and a wish. Developing a vision requires taking time and thinking about what you *specifically* want. In business, for example, this might involve reflecting on a particular team, department or company you want to build. What type of people do you see working with you? What kind of culture do you want to develop? What type of service do you want to be known for? All of these questions require very specific answers in order for you to begin the process of generating a true vision for your career.

It's no different with your personal life. Anyone who is married undoubtedly desires an outstanding and fulfilling partnership. Unfortunately, for most married couples, that is where the vision stops. They want a satisfying marriage but have not spent the time thinking through, specifically, what that would look like. Focusing on a common vision for what both people want from their marriage would be a huge step towards achieving a fulfilling partnership. As our definition illustrates, when something becomes a vision, it's not only specific but it instills passion and drives your commitment to achieve it. The same could be said for anything else that is important in our lives. Whether it's parenting our kids, learning a new skill or starting a new venture, success in any area requires the same critical element of vision, which is having a very *specific picture* of what you want.

Vision is Constantly Recurring

The next aspect of true vision is that it is "constantly recurring" in your mind. It's not just an occasional thought or a wish that something were true. It is constantly recurring either because you have developed the discipline to focus on it every day or because it is already such a part of you that you cannot help but to dwell on it. People who want to move from wishful thinking to the vision stage have to spend time every day creating a clear mental picture of what they want to achieve.

Think about the personal examples I listed earlier. Which of these individuals did not think EVERY DAY about their vision? Could they have accomplished what they did if they simply gave it occasional thought? Which of them did not have great passion and commitment to achieve their desires? Martin Luther King Jr.? George Washington? Susan B. Anthony? Bill Gates? Jackie Robinson? Every one of them focused every day on a specific vision for their life. Every one of them faced enormous obstacles that stood in their way, yet they succeeded at overcoming them. Who isn't inspired by stories of people facing a mountain in front of them only to take it on and conquer it? It makes us all believe in what is possible for ourselves if we would only face it and be clear about what we want. That's what the amazing person in the next story did and his name will remain in the record books for a very long time.

Climbing Mount Everest is a daunting feat that tests the physical limits of anyone who tries to reach the summit. To date, 223 people have lost their lives attempting the climb because of the variety of lethal conditions. Yet Yuichiro Miura of Japan has the extraordinary distinction of having climbed the peak three times. If that weren't enough, he made his first two successful climbs at age 70 and 75. The third time he ascended the peak, he was 80, which earned him the record of being the oldest person ever to climb Everest! This is what the power of vision does for a person. It drives them to take what is clear and powerful in their mind and convert it into the satisfying reality of a vision achieved.

Take a moment and do some personal reflection. Think of something in your life that you are proud of and that required a significant amount of time and effort for you to achieve. I have no doubt that as you think back through your greatest achievements, you will remember that you thought constantly about it. I'm certain that a day rarely went by that you didn't spend time dwelling on what you really wanted to achieve. This is how all great achievements occur. It doesn't matter what it is, mentally your vision takes you over.

A friend who played professional golf told me that a night rarely goes by when he does not picture himself swinging the club and playing a different course before he falls asleep. Envisioning success has become a habit for him. It doesn't matter the sport. Quarterbacks spend hours not only practicing, but also thinking through their mechanics. Tennis players do the same thing with their swings. Great musicians and artists mentally rehearse every day. Great scholars often think deeply about their subject. For whatever you want to be great at, you will have to spend time every day envisioning specifically what your goal or objective is -- and then mentally practicing the steps to achieve it. Once you have done this consciously for long enough, it will become an ingrained mental habit. It will become such a big part of you that recurring thoughts will come more naturally with less effort. Think of your brain as a muscle that must get regular (visualization) exercise to achieve its goals. Building this muscle is integral to your success.

Visualization

It's important to remember that ALL the specifics of your vision matter. One way to bring greater clarity to your vision is to use the technique of visualization. I have personally found that the best times to practice are at night when I go to bed. Before I fall asleep, it has become a habit for me to dwell on very specific images of what I want to achieve. This is something I have been doing for years.

I was an avid tennis player growing up and loved competing in tournaments. When I was 17, I was very fortunate to have found a coach named Carlos who knew exactly how the power of vision could impact a person's athletic development. Carlos was completing his Ph.D. in sports psychology and was at the forefront of new research on the close association between visual imagery and performance. I remember Carlos telling me to "see myself hitting the ball." He told me to me spend time every night before a tournament imagining myself playing a match. He told me to picture myself hitting serves and forehands and backhands and moving the ball around the court. Back then, psychologists called it "imagery." I didn't really get it at the time. But today, imagery and visualization have been confirmed as powerful tools to increase performance in competitive sports.

The same principle applies to golf. Any good sports psychologist will tell golfers to think about where they want to hit the ball, NOT where they DON'T want to hit it. I would venture that most golfers have experienced this: you get to the tee box, you see water or trees on the right and you say to yourself, "Don't hit it to the right." Amazingly, what happens? You push (or slice) your ball to the right! Your body listens to what your mind focuses on. When the idea of "the right side" is more present in your mind than the idea of "down the middle," your body will ever-so-slightly adjust to push the ball in the direction where your mind is most focused. This is the power of mental imagery.

Where your mind goes, often your behavior will follow. If I focus on having a terrific relationship with my kids, over time I will begin to act on that image naturally. If I think about being an engaging and confident leader, over time I will begin to display those qualities when I lead. People who do not take this mental work seriously will miss out on the opportunity to harness the power of their mind. The brain is an amazing machine that is designed to work for us even when we aren't consciously thinking about specific tasks or goals.

Mind-Body Interaction

Michel Chevreul was a 19th century chemist who devised an experiment that illustrated the connection between the brain's thoughts and the body's automatic and subconscious actions. You can try this experiment, called "Chevreul's Pendulum," for yourself. Take a piece of string about 8 inches long and tie a ring or a washer to it. Hold the string between your thumb and index finger with your thumb on bottom. Keep your hand perfectly still so the ring or washer is not moving. Repeat to yourself (silently or out loud) "left, right, left, right" over and over. Within seconds, you will begin to see the object moving side to side. Then start saying "round and round and round and round" repeatedly. Again, within seconds the object will start traveling in a circular motion. Whether you say clockwise, counterclockwise, up and down, side to side, it does not matter. The object will move in the direction you are thinking.

This experiment illustrates how we can create "ideomotor effects." When we think repeatedly about a movement, our body produces nerve impulses that subtly correspond to what we are thinking about. Chevreul's goal at the time was to show that the paranormal claims of charlatans were nothing more than physical-psychological interactions. In his day, spiritual "quacks" used Ouija boards, automatic writing techniques and divining rods to deceive people into believing they were having a real encounter with the supernatural. In reality, this was nothing more than a powerful mind-body connection. For our purposes, Chevreul's discovery, along with a century more of research in this field, shows that this connection between what we focus on and what we do is both real and strong. That means we can use it as a form of mental conditioning and a tool that allows our minds to work for us both consciously and subconsciously. Whether it is athletics, therapy, medicine or business, taking control of your thoughts and learning how to use them intentionally can yield remarkable rewards.

Passion and Commitment

You also know you have a real vision when it instills passion and drives commitment. Why? Because a real vision works much like an energy loop. It drives your passion and, at the same time, it feeds your passion. This is one of the reasons why some of the most famous people we respect have sustained their passion for the same things for 30, 40, even 50 years or more. We admire Martin Luther King Jr. for his relentless pursuit of equality and dignity for all men. In his famous speech he said "I have a dream…" What he could have said is, "I have a vision." That's because his dream had all the characteristics of a vision. It was specific, constantly recurring, and it instilled passion and drove his commitment to achieve it. Often, people think that real visionaries are people who have risen to public prominence like Martin Luther King Jr., Nelson Mandela or George Washington. It's true these men were incredible visionaries. But they were just normal people like you and me who found their vision and invested in it throughout the entirety of their lives.

So what is your vision? Can you answer that question immediately? If not, it's likely you have not thought about vision in quite these terms. I was much the same way for many years. I had things I loved. I had things I believed in. I was a passionate person about many things. But I never harnessed my vision into something that was specific, constantly recurring in my mind and useful for propelling me forward.

For example, I remember being awestruck by people who could speak to large crowds. I particularly admired their ability to move and persuade people through their rhetorical skills. I knew that if I wanted to develop that skill, I would have to do things I found difficult and even hated at the time. I would have to become a disciplined reader. I would have to become a lover of learning and knowledge. I would have to become excellent with the English language. And I would have to study people.

So I began the process of reading every day to prepare myself for the opportunities I believed would come my way. Every night, I would lie in bed and picture myself in front of large crowds delivering messages in which I strongly believed. It was fun. In my mind, I spoke at churches, universities, stadiums and auditoriums. Wherever I could picture a crowd, I envisioned myself dazzling audiences everywhere! These weren't hazy thoughts and vague scenarios. I would actually put together talks in my head and I would watch the audience react to everything I was saying. It was my own private ritual that helped me end my days positively and motivated for the days ahead.

I firmly believe that focusing my mind like that all those years helped better prepare me for speaking opportunities when they finally arrived. Focusing my mind intently on a particular vision allowed me to define myself by who I wanted to be and what I wanted to do. As a result, I am very fortunate to have been able to influence and impact numbers of people over the years. This would not have been possible if I just had a vague hope or wish to be a successful speaker. It required vision.

The great thing about a vision is that you can have as many as you want. You can have one for your marriage. You can have one for the type of parent you want to be. You can have a vision for your faith or even a vision for developing your talents. There are no guarantees in this life, but having a vision sure increases your odds in achieving the desires of your heart.

One of my favorite wisdom sayings in the Bible says, "The horse is prepared for battle, but victory belongs to the Lord" (Proverbs 21:31). Our responsibility is to prepare. How things end can result from things beyond our control. But if we don't prepare our horse for battle, the chance of us winning is virtually zero. Practicing vision is just one of several tools that we can use to greatly improve our chance of succeeding at whatever we desire. We should not take this lightly. Too many people stay in the realm of wishing and hoping and waiting for something to happen. However, it's the people who live life intentionally -- who know what they want and who dwell on their vision -- who are most likely to realize their dreams.

I remember talking to a client about the importance of vision. I asked him to describe to me what vision in his life looks like. I could tell he was irritated by the question, mainly because he was not able to give me more than just broad generalities. He eventually said that all this talk about vision was nice in theory, but it didn't really change anything. He said that thinking and dwelling on something won't make it happen. I listened to him rant for a bit, then finally told him that I agreed. If all you did was think about what you wanted every day, then obviously nothing would change. But that is not what I was saying. Remember, the path to achieving a dream starts with vision, but you have to follow it up with the next critical skill for successful living. That's what the following chapter will be about. You have to be able to act and take *initiative...*

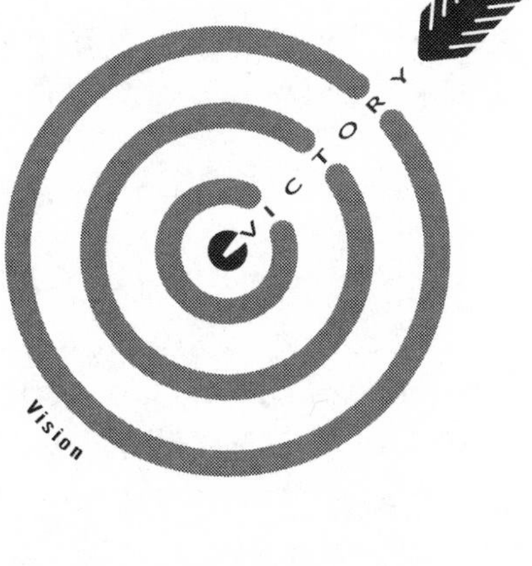

KEY POINTS

- Vision is *a specific and constantly recurring image that instills and drives your passion.*
- Focusing your mind as specifically as possible will help you to see and achieve your ultimate objectives.
- Creating mental rituals every day or every night are key to focusing the mind on achieving your vision.
- We can only prepare as effectively as our vision is clear.
- Living life intentionally is the pathway to success.

APPLICATION EXERCISES

1. Make some time to be alone without any distractions. Spend this time thinking about what is most important to you. Maybe it's financial security. Maybe it's your children. Maybe it's your spouse. Maybe it's your business. Maybe it's all of those things. Whatever they are, write down those things that you find yourself thinking about even when you are away from them.

2. Take one or two of those things and start thinking about what you would love for them to look like. Remember to be specific. What feelings do you have when you think of those things? What does the physical environment look like around you? Which people are a part of it? Flesh out the details as specifically as you can.

3. Commit every day to spending at least 10 minutes dwelling on the specifics of your vision. As you do that, ask yourself what sorts of things are required for this vision to be realized. Maybe it's more school. Maybe it's a self-study program. Maybe it's reaching out to a certain person or group. Maybe it's a discipline you have not spent much time developing. Maybe it's blocking out time in advance every week so that nothing gets in the way. Write it all down.

4. Now you are ready for the next step....

Anything goes on this page. White page brainstorming and idea creation can be very powerful—write anything that comes to mind or anything you have read that triggers your thoughts about VISION. Don't leave this page blank!

INITIATIVE

IN ORDER TO GET A PROMOTION THIS YEAR, YOU'LL JUST NEED TO SHOW LEADERSHIP INITIATIVE IN YOUR PEER GROUP.

©2014 DAVID WILBORN
THERE'S JUST ONE PROBLEM WITH THAT PLAN.

WHAT'S THAT?
I'M FUNDAMENTALLY LAZY.

“No problem is problem”

- Japanese Proverb -

TWO

THE POWER OF INITIATIVE

Have you ever met someone who consistently follows through on what they say they want to accomplish? At the same time, do you know others whose plans die the death of good intentions? People talk about making positive changes all the time. They might say they want to go back to school, start a business, lose weight, get out of debt or something as simple as "read more." In many cases, the best of plans never make it to the first steps of execution. But that's not the case with Mark.

Mark seemed to recognize from a young age that good intentions alone are not enough. Mark was one of those rare guys I knew growing up who always took initiative. He made things happen. In 9th grade, his basketball coach told him his chances of making the high school team were slim because he "wasn't quick enough and his shot was just average." Well, that was all Mark needed to hear. He began lifting weights, running and shooting baskets every day -- and I do mean every day. He worked his tail off. He knew he would never be one of the fastest or strongest guys on the team, but he was determined to have one of the best shooting records. So that's what he worked on relentlessly. After weeks of practice, it seemed that anything he threw at the basket went in. When tryouts came, Mark not only made the team, but he had a great season. That's what initiative looks like.

Mark's story was similar in baseball. His varsity coach told him he wasn't strong enough to be a big hitter. Again, Mark hit the gym and began working out every day. In a year, he got so big that he looked like a completely different person. More importantly, the effort paid off on the ball field. Not only did Mark have the highest batting average that season (over .400), but he also hit several critical home runs.

When Mark turned 20, he took all the money he had saved from mowing lawns and umpiring baseball games during his teenage years and bought his first business -- a fast food restaurant inside a gas station. He didn't just buy the enterprise and let things take care of themselves. He hired a cook and began running the business. He didn't allow fear of failure or fear of losing his money to keep him from taking action. He took initiative to make things happen. Mark is now in his mid-40s and his life's pattern is consistent. He has enjoyed a series of business successes. At the same time, his marriage of almost 20 years, his relationship with his three daughters and his spiritual faith have all prospered. The results are obvious to anyone who knows him… especially to me because Mark is my brother.

Remember the list of achievers I scribbled on the plane? Every one of these people took initiative in at least one important area of their life. None of them sat back and waited for things to happen. They acted on their vision. Vision without initiative is an unrealized dream at best. At worst, it is just wishful thinking. Dwelling consistently on what you want to accomplish won't get you to your destination, no matter how clear your goals are or how strongly you desire to see them fulfilled. There are a few things that can get in the way of taking initiative. If we can name them and understand them, we have taken a major step toward preventing them from stopping us in our tracks.

Overcoming Fear

It will come as no surprise that one of the biggest barriers to success is fear. Fear can paralyze you from taking action. It's a roadblock to success because the pursuit of virtually anything worthwhile involves risk, which elicits fear. Starting a new business is exciting, but it could fail. Investing more aggressively has great potential rewards, but you could lose your money. Having critical conversations with people could help you break through relational challenges, but there's the danger of rejection and hurt.

Many things can cause fear. We may worry about what people will think if we fail. We may believe that deep down we don't have what it takes to succeed, so we don't risk trying. The solution to overcoming fear is to develop a mindset of "no matter what." Your attitude must be one where the consequences of a dream unrealized inspire more fear than the risk of trying. This is why the roll call of highly successful people is not very long. These men and women are willing to accept the consequences of taking initiative because the consequences of unrealized possibilities are *not* acceptable.

I remember reading about a popular sports psychologist who would have people walk across a balance beam in his office. After they crossed the beam five or six times, he would ask, "Can you walk across a balance beam?" The answer was invariably "yes." He would then ask, "Could you do it again?" The answer again was "yes." Then he would take them next door to a room with a high ceiling and a balance beam hovering 10 feet in the air. He would ask them to try the exercise again. At this point, people would look up at the balance beam and reconsider their ability. When asked why they would not do what they had done easily in the other room, the reply was always the same: "Because I don't want to fall!"

This example clearly illustrates how fear has the power to impede our success. Think about this group. Each person demonstrated multiple times that they had the ability to walk across the beam. Their confidence was high until one thing changed – the risk of failure. Perhaps if padded mats were placed beneath the high beam, more people would have attempted the exercise. But the fear of falling in this case, and negative feelings induced by circumstances in our own lives, have the power to inhibit us from doing things that we are quite capable of accomplishing. You don't need to deny your fear. But you do need to understand what lies behind it. Successful people aren't fearless. They just learn to FACE their fear so it doesn't impede their success.

Be a Self-Starter

How many times have you really wanted to meet someone, but never took the initiative? Have you ever neglected to follow up on a business referral? Do you have projects that never even got off the ground? How many people do you know who said they were going to start a business and never even put pen to paper? Maybe you are one of them. Our lists of good intentions could go on and on. There wasn't a single person on my list of successful people who did not have the word "initiative" written next to their name. All of them were self-starters who took the actions required to achieve their vision.

I remember the day I decided to leave a group I was working with to start my own business. I genuinely enjoyed the people I worked with and loved being part of a great team. Frankly, it was nice to have guaranteed work and not face the stress of finding clients and proving my worth to each one. However, as life became more complicated and my financial needs became greater, I realized it was time for me to either venture out on my own or find another group to work with. When I made the decision to change direction, I did not know what lay ahead. There were a couple of potential clients who I contacted right away. By God's grace and through a lot of hard work and preparation over the years, I was able to secure work and begin the process of launching my own independent consulting business. After some other positive and unexpected events, I was thrilled (and relieved) to see that my decision was the right one.

Since that day, I have worked very hard to continue to grow my business and give the best work I possibly can to all my clients. Had I not taken the initiative to make a change and follow my vision, I would never have experienced the joy and reward of developing my own business. Though I learned this lesson later in life than my brother, I am thankful that I acted in time to fulfill a dream. A handful of individuals throughout history have demonstrated initiative to overcome even more daunting obstacles and achieve success against incredible odds.

Sarah Breedlove, later Madame C.J. Walker, was born in 1867. She faced particular challenges as the daughter of plantation slaves and as a black woman growing up amid the racial tensions and troubled times following the Civil War. If that wasn't enough, Sarah's mother died when she was five and her father, after remarrying, died one year later. Sarah married at age 20, had a daughter and then lost her husband as well. To make ends meet, she began working as a washer woman earning about a dollar a day.

Because her three brothers were barbers, Sarah developed an interest in hair care for women. In order to make more money, she started selling women's hair products for Annie Turnbo Malone and then began developing her own products. The soaps and poor-quality hygiene items of that day caused a variety of cosmetic problems for black women, so Sarah created a line of products that helped heal scalp diseases and repair damaged hair. By 1906, she had created a successful mail order business. By 1910, she had built a factory, a hair salon and a beauty school in Indianapolis to train her sales people. By 1917, she had hosted her first annual conference in Philadelphia and eventually exported her products to South America and the Caribbean. Sarah was an inspiration to many, becoming the first black female millionaire in America during a time when racial barriers made it difficult for any African American to succeed.

One of her best-known quotes is: "I am a woman who came from the cotton fields of the South. From there I was promoted to the washtub. From the washtub I was promoted to the cook kitchen, and from there I promoted myself into the business of manufacturing hair goods and preparation. I have built my own factory on my own ground."

It doesn't matter who we are talking about. If someone has shown great success in some area of life, I guarantee they have taken initiative and overcome obstacles that threatened to block their path. I can't tell you how many people I have spoken to over the years that had some absolutely terrific idea to do something. These were powerful ideas founded on solid strategies. They could have yielded tremendous benefits for this "visionary" person as well as for his or her family, customers and even society. The problem was that these individuals, as creative as they were, never followed up on their ideas.

I was recently at a restaurant in Wichita, Kansas talking to my waiter about his life and goals. He was 34, worked very hard, had great people skills and had a clear vision of the ultimate career he would like to pursue. He wanted to start a consulting business for independent restaurants and bars. He had 15 years of industry experience and he knew he could help other businesses perform better. You could see the gleam in his eyes and hear the excitement in his voice as he told me about his dream job. After he spoke, I commended his vision and asked "What's the next step?" The light went out from his eyes. He said he wished he could take that next step, but his 30-hour-a-week job was too consuming.

Well, you can imagine what I said to him at that point. I was blunt. I listed people I knew who started new careers while they were taking care of children and working full time. I told him that anyone who says that a 30-hour-a-week job is too much is using that as an excuse to avoid stepping up to the challenge. I was encouraged that he agreed. He admitted that he had not acted on his vision because he didn't know how to get started. I appreciated that. I loved the fact that he owned up to the real issue. It was lack of knowledge. To his credit he was very open to ideas. I grabbed a napkin and spent 15 minutes sketching out an initial plan for his business. I wrote out what he said he could accomplish for clients. Next, I made a list of his credentials. I finished by writing a marketing strategy that could help him secure his first client. Whether or not he decides to move forward with the plan is ultimately up to him. He will have to determine whether this is simply a wish or if it's truly a vision worth pursuing. If it's a true vision worth committing to, then having a plan will make all the difference. It will be a road map to translating intention into action, and initiative will provide the fuel.

It's important to remember that being a self-starter doesn't mean relying solely on your own resources. That's why I was eager to help my waiter with his dream. You should not be afraid to ask for help or get your hands on resources prepared by others. Ask people a lot of questions. Read. Go Online and watch educational videos. So much information is at our disposal today that there is virtually no excuse for not knowing how to get started at something. Lack of access to good information was a problem of the past. That excuse just doesn't fly today.

So think about your life for a moment. What sorts of things would you like to see? What are the most important areas of your life where you would like to make significant improvements? Whatever they are, do your best to be clear on what you want them to look like. Then get ready to act. Don't ever forget that the biggest difference between people who achieve their objectives and people who don't is often dictated by which ones take the initiative to act. Whether it's taking your business to the next level, taking your marriage to a new place or improving your health, all of these have one thing in common—**they require the ability to take initiative and start making new things happen.**

SUMMARY

KEY POINTS

- Vision without initiative is nothing more than a dream.
- The greatest obstacle to taking initiative is fear.
- Creating a compelling reason to act is the only way to overcome fear.
- Initiative must follow a clear and compelling vision.
- Being a self-starter is what is required to consistently take initiative.
- Taking initiative requires knowing what to do. Do your homework!

APPLICATION EXERCISES

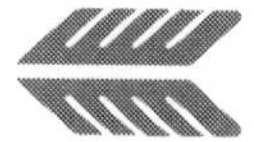

1. Think of a person you have wanted to have a conversation with but you haven't because you fear the possibility of negative consequences. Answer the following questions:

    a. What would you want to say to them? (Write it down on paper.)

    b. What possible reactions/responses might they have? (Write it down.)

    c. What do you fear from those reactions/responses? (Write it down.)

    d. Write down why taking the initiative is more important than the consequences. Be specific.

    e. Go have the conversation, fully prepared for the most negative consequence.

2. What have you wanted to do for some time that you have never gotten around to doing? Is there any element of fear connected to not taking initiative? If so, define what it is and write down the specific fears.

    a. If it's fear you don't have the resources, then make a plan to get them.

    b. If it's fear you don't have the skills necessary, then talk to some people who do have those skills and get their input or help.

c. If it's fear of failure or looking bad, then spend some time working through why that matters so much to you. Seek counsel from someone you respect to talk you through it and encourage you to take action.

3. Spend some time alone or with a person you have always wanted to work with. Begin engaging in a thought exploration session and write down some things you might be inspired to pursue. If you come up with something, write down what first steps you will need to take. Then make sure you write down deadlines to keep yourself accountable. You may be surprised at how much more you will get done by simply starting the process of taking initiative.

Anything goes on this page. White page brainstorming and idea creation can be very powerful—write anything that comes to mind or anything you have read that triggers your thoughts about INITIATIVE. Don't leave this page blank!

THE H.R. DEPARTMENT HAS JUST RELEASED A NEW **THREE HOUR** MANDATORY VIDEO TRAINING.
©2019 DAVID WILBORN

HOWEVER, YOU CAN RIGHT-CLICK THE PLAYBACK BUTTON TO RUN THE VIDEO AT DOUBLE SPEED IN THE BACK-ROUND WHILE YOU WORK,
AND THE KNOWLEDGE TEST WILL LET YOU TRY EACH QUESTION AS MANY TIMES AS NEEDED TO PASS.

WHAT'S THE TRAINING ABOUT?
CORPORATE ETHICS AND ACCURATE TIME KEEPING.

"The tongue in your mouth and the tongue in your shoe should point in the same direction"

- Southern Proverb -

THREE

YOUR CHARACTER: WHO ARE YOU?

As I was compiling my list of successful people, I knew this particular quality was going to be consistent across individuals and categories before I even started the exercise. It's the trait of *character*. We've all heard the popular definition that character is demonstrated by what you do when no one is looking. We don't respect people whose private lives are different from their public appearance. In fact when this becomes a pattern, we call such people duplicitous or hypocritical. I am not talking about perfection. None of us are perfect and few of us hold others to that standard. Being a person of character is not about living without mistakes. It's about striving to do what's right, making things right when you mess up and then moving forward.

When we think about success in any area of life, we have to recognize the role that values play. The saying "Tell me your values and I'll tell you your behavior" is true. While we don't act from our value system perfectly all the time, the ideals we hold closely inform our choices and set the path for our life. The elements of character are ingrained in us from a young age. For example, someone who grows up in an environment where money is highly valued will likely make choices based on how they affect wealth. If a person grows up with a value system oriented toward kindness, there is a strong chance they will value kindness as a character quality into their adult life. This isn't groundbreaking news. It is important, however, to address issues of character because your life's vision needs to align with your core values.

Most of us are aware that we have deeply held beliefs that guide our attitude and our actions. We might even be able to name them if we gave it thought. But it's not likely that we have taken the time to write them down. Just as businesses create organizational value statements that provide an ethical foundation for achieving their vision, so too individuals should be explicitly aware of their core values. When I wrote my core values, I determined that these were the seven things that inform my choices every day:

My Core Values

- Engaging those around me and meeting people "where they are at" rather than expecting them to adjust to my preferences
- Helping to meet the needs of others when confronted by those needs
- Growing in greater alignment between my "outer world" and my "inner world"
- Maintaining a balanced life between work and leisure
- Pursuing a life of continual learning
- Leading, teaching and developing as a way of life
- Integrating my faith beliefs in everything I do

When I am confronted with certain choices, one of these values statements is at the forefront of my mind. One might think of them as a moral compass that guides us to act consistently in alignment with our core beliefs. In fact, when I recall some of the worst decisions of my life, I can go back to my values statements and see exactly how I violated them. My seven core values may not be yours. But I promise that you have at least seven of your own that you live by every day.

Before you write your values, it is important to understand the critical distinction between said values vs. lived values. Said values are those ideals we know we *should* live by. Lived values are the ones we practice consistently. For example, you might know that showing care and concern for others is the right thing to do, but in reality you find yourself too focused on your own needs and too busy to engage the people around you. That would be an example of a *said value*. This is an important distinction to understand because when we begin listing our core values, we want to make sure we don't just write the things we think we're supposed to believe. Rather, we need to evaluate our values in light of how we actually behave. Being honest with yourself is critical here and will ensure you get the most value out of this exercise. Obviously if we want to grow and develop our values, we can write down what we think they *ought* to be. But it is essential to recognize what your lived values are. So take a few minutes and think about your regular actions and thought patterns. Think about where you spend most of your time. Think about what you spend your money on. Think about what things you enjoy doing most when you have down time. Take a few minutes and write down what your most dominant lived values are. It will require you to stop for a bit and really reflect on your daily, weekly and monthly habits, but it will be worth it.

Value Statement 1: ____

____

Value Statement 2: ____

____

Value Statement 3: ______________________________

____

Value Statement 4: ______________________________

____

Value Statement 5: ______________________________

____

Value Statement 6: ______________________________

____

Value Statement 7: ______________________________

____

The statements you have written are a significant dimension of your character. They drive the actions people observe in deciding if they can trust you and in determining the degree to which they want to help you reach your goals. It is this ethical dimension of character that is so directly connected to success in every area of your life. It will have a direct impact on the way you run your business, the way you lead your team, the way you treat your spouse and the way you raise your children. Maybe there is a critical value that you wanted to write down but couldn't. Try to discover what that value is that you believe ought to be a regular part of your life and think about what you need to do to make it a lived value.

The other critical aspect of character is related to your ability to do the hard things in order to achieve your ultimate goals. So often it's easier to just give up or stay down once you've fallen, but the person of character always gets up and believes that they can still accomplish something great. Heather Dorniden is someone who faced this very choice, took the riskier and more-challenging path, and reaped the rewards. Frankly, I've never seen anything quite like it.

Heather was a track star for the University of Minnesota. In 2008, she was running in the 600-meter race at the Big 10 Indoor Track Championships. Six hundred meters is not a terribly long distance so there isn't much room for big mistakes, especially the one Heather made. At 58 seconds into the race and leading the pack of four runners, Heather tripped and took a nasty fall resulting in an awful full face plant. With only 200 meters left and trailing behind everyone by at least 25 meters, Heather got up and began to give it everything she had again. The announcers could not believe their eyes as Heather caught up to the rest of the racers. With a sudden burst of speed, she finally slipped past the leader just before the finish line and won by less than a second. The crowd was amazed. Heather's winning time was 1 minute, 32 seconds, which meant that she only had 34 seconds to make up a 25-meter deficit and win the race.

Many runners would have quit and chalked up their defeat to an unfortunate misstep. Others may have risen to their feet and jogged to the finish line to salvage their pride. But not Heather. She ignored a stumble that could have destroyed her chances of victory. She drew from a deep inner-reserve of perseverance and physical power. She chose the harder road and passed on the easier choice to let negative circumstances define her path. This is what character is all about. This is the spirit of *character* and is the makeup of anyone who has achieved anything of great significance. All of us stumble. All of us fall down somewhere on the path of life. There's nothing we can do about that, but what we can control is what we decide to do after we fall. Unfortunately, far too many people let their setbacks and failures limit them rather than taking the harder road of learning and rebuilding.

As I was studying the word character, I found it helpful to explore how this word was used in antiquity. For example, in the ancient Hebrew Scriptures there was no word for "character" like we have in English. Our word "character" is translated from the Hebrew word "chayil" which carries the idea of having strength, might or power. Realizing this helped me better understand a second crucial dimension of character. Having character oftentimes means *having the strength to do what is right when the opportunity to do what is easier is available.* In other words, when pressed between two choices, the harder choice usually requires more strength of character. I have shared this with dozens of people and no one ever disagrees. When we see someone take the more challenging road over the easier road we do view them in a more positive light.

Think about a time when someone harmed your property or your reputation. The easy path would have been retribution. The tougher choice - the one that requires strength of character - is taking the more challenging road. Perhaps this means forgiving them. Maybe it means when their name comes up that you choose to not say anything critical of them. Whatever it is, character is clearly not built on easy decisions. Character is both built and displayed when we do the right thing no matter what obstacles and temptations we face. I know this is easier said than done. It's not easy. In fact, if we are honest with ourselves, we could come up with many examples of times that we acted or responded in ways that we are not proud of. It's not about being perfect. It's about learning through our mistakes and challenges and growing the muscles of our character. As we keep growing, we will find ourselves taking paths that we never would have taken in our past.

Not long ago I was watching the news and they showed an amazing story of a man who displayed great character. A gas station camera caught the entire incident. Several people were pumping gas when all of a sudden out of nowhere an out-of-control vehicle plowed into the gas pumps. Smoke and fire immediately erupted and all the people at the pump scattered for their lives--that is all but one. This man instinctively ran to the car that crashed into the pump and struggled to pull the unconscious driver out of his car. After he finally pulled the driver out of the car he began feverishly dragging him away from the gas pumps. Within seconds, a large explosion ensued that would have killed both of them had this hero not taken immediate action. Now I don't know anything else about this man's life, but I do know this. In that moment he displayed character as I've never seen before. He unquestionably took the hard road saving a stranger's life while risking his own.

Character and Building Trust

I once worked with a client who was a senior project manager for a large manufacturing company. He complained that his bosses did not value him. In fact, he guessed they would probably overlook him for a promotion. When I asked him to describe his relationships with the people who reported to him, he gave typical answers. He told me they worked together well and accomplished their goals every year. Shouldn't that be enough for a promotion? I asked his permission to pose three questions to him and encouraged my client to be brutally honest with his answers. He agreed. The three questions I asked him were:

1. How would your team say that you specifically demonstrate that you are *for* them? Not for your company. Not for yourself. But for *them*.

2. When was the last time you wrote a note of appreciation to any of your coworkers? If not a note, then what specifically do you do on a regular basis to express genuine appreciation for their efforts?

3. What area of leadership are you most deficient in, the one you know you need to work on regularly?

He said that apart from making sure everyone had the tools to get their job done, he doesn't do much else. He also said he had never composed a handwritten note for anyone. He quickly added that nobody does that. I said, "Why would you want to do only those things that *everyone else is doing*? How do you distinguish yourself from other leaders at your company if you do everything they do?" He nodded and agreed that he really wasn't doing anything that would set him apart for a promotion.

In answering the third question, he struggled to come up with a response. Initially he said, "Well there are so many areas I need to work on that I don't really know where to start." I told him to share just one or two. It was like pulling teeth. He quickly realized that he does not spend much time looking for ways to improve his leadership skills.

This manager hoped for a promotion. But he lacked a clear vision and he certainly wasn't taking initiative in several key areas. He wasn't showing that he supported his team. He never took the step to affirm them with a note or word of praise. And he wasn't working to grow as a leader. All of these combined to create a lack of trust, if not with those who reported to him, then at least with those who had the power to promote him. He never realized that we create opportunities by how well we build bridges of trust with those around us. Trust is everything. We hear the word all the time and we often see many examples of it around us. But it would be useful to have a simple definition that helps us put it into practice. I have a short and memorable one that I like to use regularly:

> "Trust is the degree to which people believe you are *for them*."

It's that simple. If you want to develop a greater level of trust with people in any area of your life, they have to be convinced that you are "for them." That means they believe you are looking out for their interests just as much as your own. Trust is not only a key aspect of character but it is the "currency" of leadership and success, not just in the business world but in all areas of life. Think about the people you trust the most. It wouldn't take long for you to answer why you trust them. For example, try this exercise. Write down three names of the most trustworthy people you know. Next to their names, write the reasons why these people made it to the top of your list. Be sure to be as specific as possible.

Person 1: ______________________________

____

Person 2: ______________________________

____

Person 3: ______________________________

____

Chances are high that what you wrote down next to each person's name would qualify them as demonstrating that they are "*for you.*" In fact, I would venture to say that no one would make it on that list unless you were certain they stood behind you and had your best interests at heart. Earning the trust of others is a vital element of success, so it would serve us well to take a moment to understand how to really grow in this area.

5 Elements of TRUST

In my experience of working with individuals and organizations on improving their effectiveness and performance, I have found there to be five critical elements to effectively build trust. To make them easy to remember, I have put them into an acronym that spells "TRUST." If any one of these five elements is missing, there will eventually be a breakdown of trust. People will hesitate to fully extend their trust which can make it more difficult for you to achieve your vision. Let's take a look at these elements:

Tasks
(You are competent and knowledgeable about what you are doing.)

Reliable
(You do things on time and you do what you say you will do.)

Understanding
(You show empathy and concern for the people around you.)

Support
(You regularly offer help to others.)

Thankful
(You show gratitude and appreciation on a consistent basis.)

Let's look at each of these a little more closely and see why they are such powerful trust builders.

Competence

Working with someone who *knows their job well* **(tasks)** obviously helps us trust them more in the workplace. They don't require a high level of oversight and we can rely on their judgment and decisions. Imagine working with someone you *didn't* believe knew their job well. You might think they were a nice enough person, but that doesn't mean you would trust them with an important task. That is why *trust is directly connected to their competence.*

Consider this on a personal level. I have a friend, Jonathan, who is married to a great girl. She is an all-around "doer." She loves to work on projects around the house and thinks it's a waste of money to pay people to do what she or her husband could manage. Jonathan, however, is not exactly what you would call a handy man. His attempts at fixing things sometimes create the need for more repairs! Now, his wife loves him very much. She also trusts him when it comes to being a good husband. Her problem is not on the moral end of the scale. It's on the *task* end. She doesn't trust him to fix things around the house because he doesn't really take the time to learn how to improve as a handyman. This has resulted in quite a bit of tension between them over the years. Because of this tension, it's critically important that they do all that they can to demonstrate to each other that they are "for one another." For Jonathan it would mean taking the time to learn how to be more helpful around the house. He could possibly have a friend that is a handyman come over and begin showing him some things. Maybe he could begin watching videos on-line that would help him learn more. Doing something like this would communicate to his wife that he actually does care and that he really is for her. For his wife, building trust would involve her learning to appreciate her husband more and affirm his strengths and not make a big deal about his deficiencies. The result would be that he would begin feeling more like his wife is on his team and the planks of trust could begin to be built.

You get the point. Being competent at work or at tasks in your personal life is a great way to demonstrate to others that you know what you are doing. It shows that others have every reason to trust you. If you know you aren't very competent at some things that are important for your job or to your relationships, it is up to you to close the competence gap. Otherwise, you will continue to struggle with the consequences of not being fully trusted.

Being Reliable

Beyond being competent, you must also demonstrate that you are ***reliable***. That means people can depend on you because you do what you say you will do. Others don't have to worry about you missing deadlines or forgetting important details. If you are competent at your job but not reliable, the level of trust that others have in you will diminish. To be viewed as trustworthy, you must show people they can depend on you to accomplish what needs to be done.

At work, dependability is demonstrated by arriving at work on time, putting in a full day of work, showing up to meetings on time, participating in those meetings, not using your phone or laptop while people are talking, turning in reports when they are due, taking the time to listen so there is no confusion about expectations and, ultimately, doing what you say you are going to do -- without excuse. All of these examples are critical to being viewed as a reliable person in the workplace.

On a personal level, reliability can be demonstrated by calling people back in a reasonable amount of time, keeping private matters private, being available when people need your help, paying people back on time, returning things to people you have borrowed from and keeping your promises.

I can remember a painful event many years ago that taught me a valuable lesson on reliability. When I was in graduate school, I had a bad habit of ending my conversations with the phrase, "Great to see you. I'll give you a call!" It was just my way of concluding a conversation. I never really thought about what I was saying. One day, when I was walking from class with my good friend Wyatt, I mentioned that a group of us were going country dancing and suggested that he join us. Wyatt asked where and I replied, "I'm not exactly sure, but I'll give you a call." You can probably guess what happened. I did go dancing with my friends, but without Wyatt. I never called.

When Wyatt found out about the evening, he called and left me a voice mail I will never forget. He told me that I was not a man of my word and that he felt that I lacked integrity because I never followed up with him. Wow! Talk about painful. That was definitely a wake-up call. I immediately phoned Wyatt and asked for his forgiveness. I told him he was exactly right. There was no excuse for saying I would do something and then not follow through. It didn't matter that "I'll give you a call" was my catch-phrase to end a conversation. What ultimately mattered was that if I was going to have a good trusting relationship with Wyatt, I needed to be true to my word. Wyatt helped me learn the important truth that trust requires being reliable. This is an area that I have improved in drastically because of Wyatt's willingness to "shoot straight" with me about the importance of doing what you say you are going to do.

So how about you? In what areas of your life do you consider yourself very reliable? In what areas would you say you need to focus on more? There's no better method to become more self-aware than to write these things down and evaluate where you need to grow more. So take a moment and answer the questions below and circle your answer:

1. I am very punctual.

   ☐ Yes ☐ No ☐ Sometimes

2. I always do what I say I'm going to do.

   ☐ Yes ☐ No ☐ Sometimes

3. The tasks that I complete rarely have mistakes.

   ☐ Yes ☐ No ☐ Sometimes

4. I always follow up with people who are going through a difficult time.

   ☐ Yes ☐ No ☐ Sometimes

5. I prepare well and am a great planner.

   ☐ Yes ☐ No ☐ Sometimes

6. I am very organized with money.

☐ Yes ☐ No ☐ Sometimes

7. I always look for ways to help people in need.

☐ Yes ☐ No ☐ Sometimes

8. I always keep what people say in confidence.

☐ Yes ☐ No ☐ Sometimes

9. I always follow the rules.

☐ Yes ☐ No ☐ Sometimes

10. I can always be trusted to give honest feedback.

☐ Yes ☐ No ☐ Sometimes

These are just a few examples of what being reliable looks like. If you answered 'no' or 'sometimes' to any of them, there is room for improvement. Having to work on your reliability may not feel like fun, but the rewards are great. George MacDonald once said, "To be trusted is greater than to be loved." When we are trusted and viewed as reliable, it says something about our character and there are few things as complimentary as someone saying that we have good character.

Understanding Others

The next critical quality that builds trust in both your professional and personal life is the practice of regularly displaying care and concern for the people around you. In other words, taking the time to ***understand*** where others are coming from. Stephen Covey, in his popular book *The 7 Habits of Highly Effective People*, called this the habit of *"seeking first to understand before you seek to be understood."* You make yourself available for people to open up and share what is going on with them. This is a surprisingly rare gift to others, as few actually practice it.

Think about the closest people in your life. Most likely they have that relationship precisely because you can share things with them that you can't share with anyone else. This is the quality of *showing understanding and empathy towards others.* I can easily recall all the people in my life who have displayed this quality during times when I was going through significant challenges. All of us can. Think of a time when someone in your life, at just the right moment, took the time to listen and be there. There is no doubt in my mind that this caused your trust in them to grow significantly. When given the choice to work with people who truly care about others versus working with people who care only about doing their job, I have no doubt that the majority of people would pick working with people who care. Our closest friends are typically our closest friends precisely because they offer something that most others do not. Displaying understanding and empathy is a powerful act towards building deeper trust with the people around you.

In 2002, when I was going through a particularly difficult time in my life, I met someone who turned out to be one of my closest friends. I was speaking that summer at a camp in Oklahoma. In the audience was Matt, someone whose affirming words and demonstration of genuine concern sparked an enduring relationship. You'll hear more about Matt and the critical role he played in my life in Chapter 5, but for now just know that Matt offered exactly what I needed at that time. He offered an incredible listening ear and a deep-seated belief in me as a person. Matt repeatedly told me how bright my future was and that he was confident great things were ahead for me someday. I'm not sure if Matt knew it at the time, but those words were exactly what I needed to hear. He took the time to really understand where I was and what I needed. We ended up talking almost every day for a year. This remarkable friendship was built through acts of genuine care and concern. I'm sure all of us can think of a time when someone played a key role in our lives during a particularly difficult period. The result is nearly always a strengthening in the level of mutual trust.

So, today's questions are, "How often do you take the time to really show genuine care and concern for others?" And more specifically, "For whom have you played an instrumental role during a critical time?" Take a moment to think about it. These are important questions you should take seriously.

Offering Support

Consider the person who not only shows understanding and empathy, but also spends their time offering ***support***. This is a person who takes the time to help those around them even if it interferes with their own work. We might categorize these individuals as "ultimate team players." They see work as more than just getting their own tasks done. It's about pitching in together and everyone succeeding -- and they are willing to do their part. When considering what a supportive attitude looks like in action, I can't help but think of my friend Dan. I've moved three times over the past several years and each time I called Dan, he never hesitated to help me lug my stuff to a new place. I can't think of a single time when I've needed something and Dan has not been there. He even takes the initiative before I ask. He has called me many times to ask if I needed any help. As a result, I firmly believe that Dan is *for me*.

Another person who comes to mind when I think of support is my next door neighbor, Bill. You could not ask for a better neighbor. Bill is one of those guys who owns every tool known to man. He has told me many times, "My garage is your garage. Whatever you need, just go in and grab it." Now that would be neighborly enough, except that Bill comes over all the time to fix things for my wife and me. He's fixed our refrigerator, he's fixed our toilets and he's mowed our lawn. Time and again, he's offered to fix countless things at our house.

One day I mentioned to Bill that my wife and I wanted to pull out several large bushes from the front of our house so we could do some landscaping. The next morning at 9 a.m., Bill had his Ford F-250 pickup truck loaded with chains and ropes ready to rip those bushes out of the ground. A few hours later, eight large bushes had been removed and we ended up saving quite a bit of money. Now that's what you call offering support!

Being supportive is not just about hard physical labor, such as helping people move or ripping bushes from the ground. It can be anything that is perceived by others as helpful. Maybe it's loaning or buying someone a book on a topic that is relevant to their life at that time. Maybe it's offering to help someone finish a work project that has been particularly time consuming. Maybe it's offering to watch your friend's kids one night so he and his wife can have a date. If you thought about it, you could come up with dozens of ways to be supportive towards others. The point is that when we lend a hand and serve others with no strings attached, a level of trust grows naturally. We just need to take the time to consider ways in which we can do things for people. This shows that we are not just looking out for ourselves but that we are *for them*, as well.

Thankfulness and Gratitude

Finally, consider the person who regularly shows appreciation and gratitude to everyone they work with. They don't just look at someone and say "thanks." They offer sincere words of gratitude. They may say something like, "Hey I want to thank you for taking a few moments to help me out. It made things so much easier for me and I wanted you to know how much I appreciate you." It may take an extra 5 seconds, but notice the difference in the level of gratitude. Showing thankfulness and appreciation on a regular basis builds trust with people because they respect the fact that you would take the time to recognize the supportive efforts of everyone around you. As trust builds, eventually you will find that gratitude will drive people to want to be more generous with their time and resources to help you when you need it.

Think of a time when you did something for someone and they showed sincere appreciation for what you did. I have no doubt that you would be much more likely to help them again if they asked you. However, if they didn't show any real gratitude, you might still help them because that is the kind of person you are, but you probably wouldn't be as motivated to do it. That's because thankfulness and gratitude build trust. For example, what if a friend was struggling financially one month and you gave them some money as a gift to help with some of their responsibilities. If all your friend said to you was "thanks!" then I suspect you might be somewhat disappointed. Compare that to a scenario where your friend mails you a note of sincere appreciation. He didn't have to do that, but the fact that he took the time to show his thankfulness would mean a lot to you. If in the future he was in need again, you would probably be just as willing to help. The reason is really simple. We all appreciate appreciation. It's not that we need to have it to help people. It's just that it motivates us to want to continue to help someone when a need arises because our trust towards them has grown.

The Handwritten Note

One of the most powerful forms of appreciation is the handwritten note. That's because when we receive a personal note, we know it took time and effort. We usually keep these expressions of gratitude and put them somewhere for safekeeping. Voice mails are nice, but they get deleted. Emails are good, but they eventually get lost among the thousands of other messages we receive. Verbal appreciation is also always nice, but it can be forgotten. The form of appreciation that really lasts and demonstrates an exceptional personal touch is the handwritten note. I encourage all my clients to stretch themselves in this area. Writing short notes doesn't take a lot of time and the reward far exceeds the effort. Even if you made yourself write one note a month, by the end of the year you would have created a dozen personalized forms of recognition that will have a lasting impact on those who receive them. Give it a try and see.

I remember a coaching session I conducted at a manufacturing site with an employee who had been there for nearly 30 years. His name was Jack and he had a good reputation for being a hard worker. However, he was not exactly known as "Mr. Recognition." I asked if there was anyone at work who he really appreciated and respected and who had helped him out recently. He immediately named one of his coworkers and shared how much this guy had helped him. I pulled out a piece of paper and said to Jack, "If you were to personally express your appreciation, write down what you would say."

He felt a little awkward, but he wrote down a very nice four- or five-sentence note. I grabbed an envelope and put his note inside. Then I challenged him to go to his coworker's office and put it on his desk if he was not there. If he was there, then Jack was to wait until he was out of his office. After he warmed up to the idea, Jack walked over to the office and left his note on the desk. Later that day, Jack came to tell me that the recipient of the note called him after reading it. His initial response was, "Jack, what the hell is this you put on my desk?" Jack said he was a little embarrassed, but he again expressed his specific feelings of gratitude. The next thing this man said to Jack made it all worth it. He said, "I've been working here almost 30 years and *no one* has ever given me a handwritten note saying thanks. This means a lot. Thank you." Home run!

Imagine how great it would be to work with someone who demonstrates all of these trust-building qualities. They know their job, they are reliable, they show understanding and concern for others, they regularly offer support and they show sincere gratitude toward everyone around them. What would it be like to have people like that as your coworkers? I remember asking this question to an audience and a lady in the back yelled out, "I have *no* idea!" Everybody cracked up. It was funny because most people do a couple of these trust elements well, but very few do all five of them well. It would be amazing to be surrounded by people who took all five trust builders seriously. Essentially, what I have described in these five aspects of trust is what character in the workplace looks like. Yet the principles apply to all relationships at work and at home.

Remember, character is the strength to do what is right when the opportunity to do what is easier is right in front of you. It's easier not to write that note or letter of appreciation. It's easier not to take the time to show concern for people around you when you are busy. It's easier not to offer support to others when you have a ton on your plate. What takes character is *having the strength to do those things anyway because they are the right things to do.*

KEY POINTS

- Character is making the choice that requires more strength rather than choosing the easier option.
- Character builds the bridge of TRUST with others.
- Character is ultimately derived from the internal values that direct one's life.
- The bridge of trust is built at work by knowing your job, being reliable, showing care and concern for others, offering support to help others in need and demonstrating real gratitude and appreciation.

APPLICATION EXERCISES

Take a few moments and answer the following questions:

1. How competent are you in your job? What would others say if asked the same question about you?
2. Other than on-the-job learning, what else do you do to be more competent?
3. How dependable are you?
    a. Are you punctual?
    b. Do details slip by sometimes?
4. Are you known as someone who takes time to show care and concern?
    a. Write down a couple of recent examples.

    ____

    ____

    ____

5. How often do you take the initiative to offer support to others?
    a. Write down a couple of recent examples.

    ____

    ____

    ____

    ____

6. Do you show sincere gratitude on a regular basis?

   a. Think of two people who deserve handwritten notes. Write notes and send them.

   b. In what other ways have you shown genuine gratitude to people?

   ____

   ____

   ____

   ____

7. Pick 10 people you know and hand them an envelope with one question to answer. Ask them for honest and direct feedback to the question: "What one thing could I do to improve further as a person?" When you get all the responses, look to see if there are any patterns. Does more than one person provide the same or similar response? Focus on those areas.

DREAM WALL

Anything goes on this page. White page brainstorming and idea creation can be very powerful—write anything that comes to mind or anything you have read that triggers your thoughts about CHARACTER. Don't leave this page blank!

TIME MANAGEMENT

"Lack of direction; not lack of time is the problem. We all have 24 hours!"

- Zig Ziglar

FOUR

TIME MANAGEMENT: DO YOU KNOW YOUR SPENDING HABITS?

One of the most fulfilling things I like to do is select a book and lead a discussion through the text with a group of guys. For several years, I met weekly with 10-12 guys and discussed 10 books in the course of that year. The discussions were awesome. Watching the men expand their knowledge and ability to think critically was truly rewarding. However, the greatest satisfaction came later when the participants began to apply what they learned. One of the best and most inspiring examples involved my friend Greg.

Greg worked for a software technology company and never really thought much about continuing his education. One day I suggested that he consider going back to school and getting his master's degree in philosophy. I never thought he would actually follow through, but he did. In fact, he got accepted into a highly-regarded program in California. One day, just three months before classes started, Greg asked if I would recommend some reading to boost his confidence. I recommended a nine-volume series on the history of philosophy, but suggested that he just read volume one since time was short and each book was well over 350 pages. To my amazement, two months later Greg told me he had finished *all nine* volumes!

I couldn't believe it. Greg told me that he put himself on a 100-page-a-day program and finished the entire series in less than two months. Greg entered his graduate program and finished with honors. After graduation, he was accepted into another graduate program in philosophy at Oxford University. Greg's whole life changed because of one very specific skill: Greg knew how to manage his time extremely well. This allowed him to focus almost exclusively on what was important to him. The result was several amazing accomplishments that most people would only dream of.

Though Greg's path is not for everyone, there are many people who exercise the same type of time management discipline and accomplish goals that are just as impressive. In my experience, the people who have achieved the greatest amounts of success in their lives have managed their time better than everyone else. This applies to family as well as professional goals. Great marriages do not just happen. Great marriages happen because two people decide to manage their time effectively to create the quality of marriage they desire. They block out time every day to talk. They schedule weekly dates. They commit to reading great books on marriage and relationships. They spend time with other couples who help strengthen their marriage. Likewise, great parenting doesn't just happen. It takes focused time.

> "It takes a quantity of time, not just quality time, because quality time is found *in* quantity time."

Going for walks, attending sports practices and games, and participating in school programs are all examples of investing time in what is important. How about being a great athlete? That doesn't just happen either. An athlete's talent may get them through their teenage years. But to compete with the best in college and beyond, you must be willing to put in the time required to achieve top-tier status.

I played competitive tennis through high school and college. Although I never broke any records, I remember learning early on that if I wanted to compete at a high level I had to put in the time. I can recall winters practicing outside when it was in the 20s and sometimes the courts were even glazed with ice. I remember the bitter wind slicing through my clothes like a knife. I knew that during the winter, a lot of players would be taking it easy. Because I started taking tennis seriously a little later than most of the really good players, I knew that the cold months would provide an opportunity to gain an edge. I've never regretted all the hours I spent practicing, eating right and working out, even when it felt miserable. I knew that it came down to how I prioritized my time to focus on what was really important. The fact is that this is true for anything that we do.

In college one season, we had a tennis practice t-shirt that read:

> "If it is to be, it is up to me."

Such a simple statement was loaded with wisdom. Enough with the excuses! There are always reasons for why we didn't do something or why we didn't accomplish some important goal. But the bottom line is that we just didn't do it. Sure there were extenuating circumstances, but that's life. We must embrace the truth that growth and achievement are rooted in the belief that "*if it is to be, it is up to me.*" Period. Who else is responsible for success? No one. Only you. That's the truth that is the heart of great success. No excuses. Unfortunately there are many people who prefer to blame their lack of success on all sorts of reasons other than themselves. The bottom line is that they are doing nothing more than coming up with excuses.

John Singleton's story is an inspiration to anyone who has ever had a dream and was tempted to let obstacles become excuses. John works at Advanced Electrical Varnishes, driving a forklift and mixing chemical compounds to create waterproof coating for wiring and circuit boards. It's a full time job that occupies John's time from 8 a.m. to 4:30 p.m. But John's day doesn't end when he leaves the plant.

Every day after work, John goes to the local golf course and practices until it's too dark to play. He has had a passion for the game for years and even traveled from his home in England to the United States to attend a two-year golf college. His progress was interrupted, however, when damage to both his knees required six surgeries which kept him off the golf course for three years.

But John lived by the maxim "If it is to be, it is up to me." With a full-time job and two bad knees, John managed his time and his emotional outlook to achieve something extraordinary. He played the qualifier tournament at Royal Liverpool in England and qualified for the British Open on his first try. I wish I could have been there when John was walking through the course with PGA greats John Daly and Dustin Johnson, two American pros who had no idea about Singleton's story. Johnson asked Singleton as they walked, "Do you play on the European Tour?" "No," said Singleton, "I work in a factory."

That's an example of someone who knew what was important and stayed laser-focused on his goal. I've observed over the years that there are three common reasons why the majority of people don't accomplish what they want. They ultimately don't spend their time focusing on what's important because they struggle with one or more of the following:

- Prioritizing poorly
- Procrastinating
- Planning ineffectively

I remember hearing someone say:

> "Most people don't lead their lives, they accept their lives."

That is a very powerful statement. It emphasizes that too many people view their life as something that happens *to them*. It says they have little control over the final outcome when, actually, we all have the ability to take control and lead ourselves toward a destination of our choosing. Of course things happen in life that can cause setbacks or even stop us completely in our tracks. However, most people still have the ability to choose how things will turn out.

Setting Priorities After Setbacks

For some who have experienced painful setbacks or failures in life, setting priorities may seem very hard to do. Let me say again, setting priorities is important in *every* stage of your life. Setting priorities after a setback is just as essential to your moving forward as it was before your setback. It doesn't matter if you recently filed for bankruptcy, went through a divorce or were let go from work. The bottom line is that the same rules apply no matter what. You cannot afford to be complacent. You have to be able to regroup, think about what you want and then develop the plan to get there. All of us love stories of people who experienced incredible loss yet were still able to pull it together and achieve something incredible. This is the power that comes from being captivated by a compelling passion in your life.

I know in my own life what it's like to be going in one direction when all of a sudden the floor falls out from under you. Sometimes it's things that happen to you. Other times it's our own choices that require us to pay a heavy toll. Regardless, it does you no good to stay defeated and let life pass you by. You still have the power to decide what you want your life to look like and make consistent choices that align with your ultimate objectives. Again, the same rules that applied prior to your setback apply after your setback. One of these rules is *the rule of prioritization.* Prioritization keeps you from procrastinating on what's important.

Prioritize for Results

One of the major reasons people put off doing the important things is because they have not established in clear-and-certain terms what matters most to them. I cannot stress enough the importance of writing down your key priorities. Doing this makes where you spend your time more clear which, in turn, will minimize your procrastination. Consider the person who goes to Walmart without a list compared to someone who goes with a list. Who will get in and out quicker? It's no different in our day-to-day life. Writing down your priorities will keep you focused more closely and help you get things done faster.

See how well you know what your key priorities are in each area of your life. Complete the exercise below as quickly as possible by answering the following questions.

In each key area of your life, write down your top priority:

Work: ______________________________

Manager/Leader: ______________________________

Spouse: ______________________________

Parent: ______________________________

Finances: ______________________________

Spiritual life: ______________________________

Education: ______________________________

So how did you do? Were you able to write down your top priority in each of these areas? For most people it's not that easy. Knowing your priorities so well that you can write them down quickly says a lot about how clear they are for you. If you found yourself struggling, it is possible that you are not exactly sure what they should be. This might be because you think you have so many that it's hard to select just one. Or you may know what's important, but it's hard to put this into words. Regardless, all of us should be able to clearly communicate one major priority in all the important areas of our life. I encourage you to spend additional time exploring and identifying your priorities in each of the key areas featured in the exercise. The answers will help keep you focused and away from the distractions life throws at you.

For many who prioritize poorly, it's not a question of laziness. Rather, it's simply that they spend too much time on the wrong things. For example, if writing a book by a certain date is important to someone, they need to dedicate time every day to write -- as tempting as it might be to avoid the hard tasks by organizing files and engaging in busywork. Trust me, I know. As I have been working on writing this book, I have been tempted by many distractions. It's not that I am being lazy. In fact, I am usually doing something that at some point needs to get done ... just not right then.

> "The problem is prioritization, not laziness."

It's likely the same with you. Organizing your office is a good thing. The question is whether that would interfere with a higher-level priority, one linked to your ultimate goals. This is a common problem. Our intentions are good and we have our priorities in mind. But it's easy to let other things get in the way.

Procrastination Chokes out Prioritization

Another reason people don't focus intently on what's important is because they *procrastinate*. I can't think of a more common and yet more toxic behavior that hinders achievement than procrastination. Jerry is a guy I began coaching about three years ago. When he and I sat down to go over his expectations and his vision of success, one thing he mentioned was that he wanted to lose 40 pounds. I thought that was a great target so we devised a plan that he agreed to follow for the next month until he saw me again. When we met the following month, Jerry hadn't even started the plan. He said he meant to, but he got sidetracked right away by a trip that interrupted his schedule. I told him I understood so we tweaked his plan to accommodate unforeseen interruptions. To make a long story short, Jerry followed through on our plan for a few days then got derailed again.

At the end of that year, he had actually *gained* ten pounds. He was embarrassed and said there was no way he would let that happen again. We set some new goals and made a new plan only to end up exactly where we started, again. It's been three years now and Jerry hasn't even gotten off the ground. His biggest problem is that he allows procrastination to get the best of him. If he says he is going to get up early to walk, he puts it off to walking at lunch. Once lunch comes, he pushes it off to walking in the evening after dinner. Guess what happens after dinner? You got it. He is tired and just wants to relax and go to bed. I'm not down on Jerry at all. I know he wants very badly to lose that weight and feel better. But for me and for so many others, procrastination is like a toxin that poisons our ability to succeed.

The bottom line about procrastination is that unless we believe that we *have to* accomplish something, it's very easy to put things off. As long as obligations stay at the level of "ought to" or "should," it's likely that we won't do what we say we want to do. The most successful people overcome procrastination by changing their mindset into a *must*, not just an *ought*. Tony Robbins is famous for saying "You have to quit should-ing on yourself and live in the world of *must*!" So what things do you believe you *must* do? What do you absolutely *have to do*? What compelling reasons do you have to overcome procrastination? Take a moment and write down the things that you believe are in the category of "Have To." Once you write them down, write your compelling reasons that make each one a "Have To" and not just an "Ought To."

"Have to" Inventory:

I have to ________________________________

I have to ________________________________

I have to ________________________________

I have to ________________________________

I have to ________________________________

I have to ________________________________

The third common reason so many people do not achieve their objectives is because *they do not plan effectively*. Abraham Lincoln was famous for saying that if he had six hours to chop down a tree, he would spend four hours sharpening his ax. That is a great example of planning and preparation. Most people would start swinging at the tree and realize too late that their ax was dull, thereby adding additional hours to the chore. Many of us approach life in much the same way. We want great things, but we haven't done a great job with planning.

I have a client and friend who is one of the most effective planners I have ever met. When he was promoted to manage a large work site, he immediately began creating a plan to ensure his success. When I asked to see his plan, he handed me a 15-page, color-coded document covering every aspect of what he would be working on that year. It was like a work of art, perfectly laid out with every detail accounted for. Needless to say, over the course of the next 12 months, his accomplishments elevated his professional reputation to "rockstar" status.

I'm not saying that everyone has to plan like this, but ineffective planning has prevented far too many people from achieving their goals. Considering how much is written on the importance of writing out your goals, you would think it would be common practice. But it isn't. Several years ago, I began the practice of writing out my goals and outlining my plans to achieve them. I can say from personal experience that the difference in my productivity and effectiveness has been significant. Every week, I sketch out plans and ideas on how to get better results from what I am doing. Whether I'm on a plane, or sitting at my desk or doing some work at a nearby Starbucks, I am constantly writing out my plans for all of the projects that I am currently working on. I lived for many years without taking planning seriously, and now I have lived many years with making it a part of my life. Believe me, the difference in results is enormous.

So what about you? Would you consider yourself a good planner? If so, what does planning look like for you? Where do you put all your plans once you write them out? How often do you look over them and review their status? All of these are critical questions to effective planning. If you take them seriously, I assure you that you will not be disappointed.

So, take a few minutes before you move on to the next chapter and list a few of the objectives that you want to accomplish. Once you write them down, take some time, and even if you think you know what you need to do, write out your plan:

Objective 1: ______________________________

____

____

Objective 2: ______________________________

____

____

Objective 3: ______________________________

____

____

Objective 4: ______________________________

____

____

I can't tell you how important this simple exercise of putting your objectives in writing is. Next, make the time to craft your plan on how to get there. Don't skip this. It's one of the practices of high achievers!

KEY POINTS

- Managing your time is within your control.
- Poor prioritization is a major reason for poor time management.
- Procrastination is a poison that hinders achievement.
- Effective planning significantly increases your likelihood of success.
- "Have To" vs. "Ought To." What are your "Have To's?"

APPLICATION EXERCISES

1. Take out your calendar and look at your last 30 days. Take an inventory of the time you spent in each major area of your life. For example, if health/fitness is one of your priorities, how did you do the past 30 days? Total up the amount of time you spent on fitness activities. Do the same thing for all the other important areas of your life.

2. Have an honesty session with yourself when it comes to the time busters that can seriously interfere with your time management. Ask yourself:

   a. Do I get distracted by less important things that keep me from focusing on what is important? List some examples.

   ____

   ____

   ____

   ____

   b. Is procrastination a problem? Are there things right now that you could have accomplished already, but you have waited? If so, what are they? When will you commit to getting them done?

   ____

   ____

   ____

   ____

   ____

   c. Create a planning document for yourself that is customized just for you and your activities. Make sure it incorporates daily, weekly and monthly objectives.

3. Decide what you *must* do. Write these things down and then come up with your plan to achieve them by a certain date. Keep this in front of you so that it is always on your mind.

D R E A M W A L L

Anything goes on this page. White page brainstorming and idea creation can be very powerful—write anything that comes to mind or anything you have read that triggers your thoughts about TIME MANAGEMENT. Don't leave this page blank!

OPTIMISM

THE PESSIMIST
THE GLASS IS HALF EMPTY.
©2014 DAVID WILBORN

THE OPTIMIST
THE GLASS IS HALF FULL.

THE PRAGMATIST
I WISH THAT WAS A BEER.

“A pessimist sees the difficulty in every opportunity; an optimist sees the opportunity in every difficulty.”

- Winston Churchill

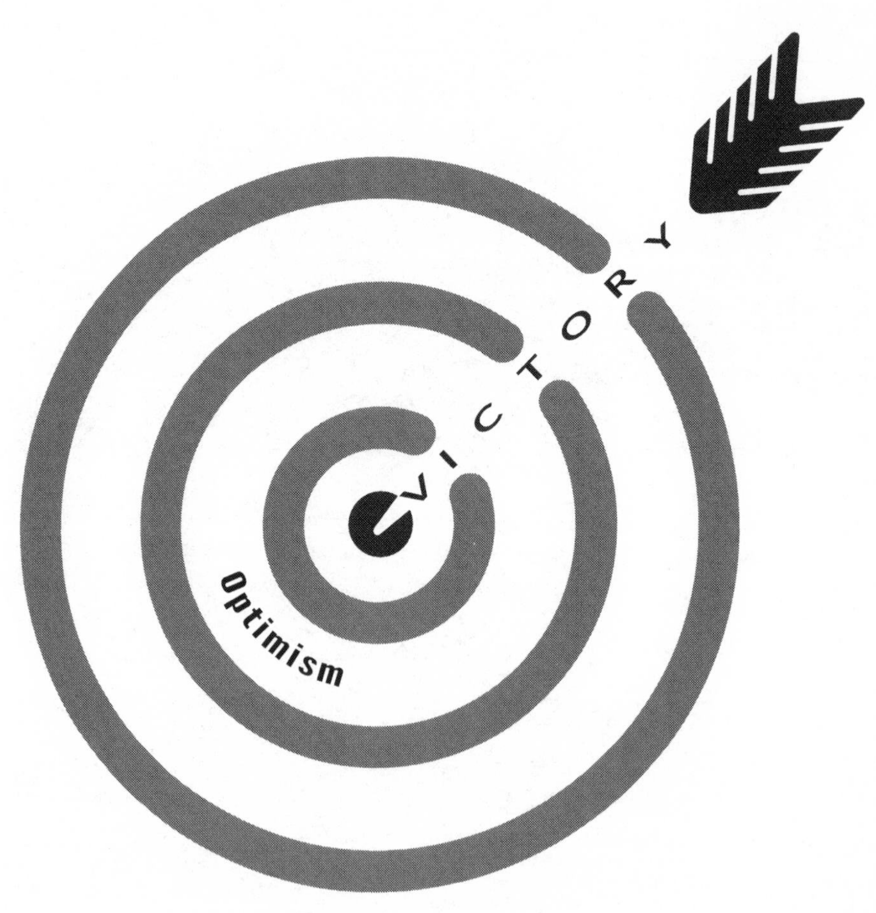

FIVE

OPTIMISM: WHAT DOES YOUR TOMORROW LOOK LIKE?

Have you ever met one of those people who always believes that things will work out? You know the type. You rarely hear them complain because they keep a positive outlook on life no matter what circumstances they face. When things don't go their way, they put on a smile and go on with their day, focusing on things that are within their control. It's not that they live in denial. Rather, they have learned that there is no benefit in allowing their circumstances to control their emotional well-being.

A recent study of people over the age of 75 asked what they would do differently in life if they could do it all over again. The number one answer was "I would have worried less." Isn't that great? The elderly survey participants realized the same thing we can understand today, without having to age and look back with regret. When we consider all the things we have feared, we realize that much of what we worried about *never* happened. I love the quote by Mark Twain when he said, "I've lived through some terrible things in my life and some have actually happened."

Isn't that so true? More than that, what does worry change? Nothing. What does worry positively add to our lives? Nothing. This is the reality of the optimist. It's not that they don't take issues in their life seriously. It's simply that they don't dwell on what they can't change. They know that given time, most obstacles will be overcome.

I can think of some of the most painful times of my life and how easy it would have been for me to dwell on how bad things were. Don't get me wrong. I wept and felt the pain at the time. But that is very different from dwelling on the negative and believing that things won't change. One of the great lessons of life I have learned is that although sometimes things can never go back to how they were, circumstances can still turn out positive or at least get measurably better. It's a matter of perspective. Optimism is a choice. We can either choose to believe that things will never get better or we can choose to believe that, in time, things will change and will even improve.

I can't help but think of one of the great people of the 20th century who embodied the essence of this truth. His name is Viktor Frankl. Frankl lived through some of the worst circumstances imaginable during the Holocaust years of World War II. Yet when the war was over, he taught millions of people a very simple truth about dealing with suffering and struggle. It all comes down to decision. How do we want to choose for things to look? We all have the ability to rise above the conditions around us by choosing what our attitude and perspective will be.

Matt is a friend of mine whose optimism is contagious. I firmly believe that he was brought into my life at exactly the right time. It was the darkest and most difficult period of my life and it took every bit of energy and discipline to keep my chin up. I met Matt while I was speaking for a week at a camp in Oklahoma. One day after hearing me speak, Matt felt compelled to introduce himself. We connected immediately and soon became the best of friends. What I found so appealing about Matt was that he was grounded in reality, yet profoundly optimistic. He shared much of his own biography and the challenges he had faced over the years. Yet he remained hopeful and convinced that his best days lay ahead.

Matt would often say to me that it was just a matter of time before

I began to experience unbelievable opportunities. He believed in me 100%. Sometimes he said such positive and encouraging things that I honestly wondered if Matt was delusional. It sometimes sounded too good. One night, we were sitting at an IHOP restaurant at 1 o'clock in the morning talking about the future. I remember Matt looking at me and saying, "Walter, you have no idea how great your future is going to be. You are going to have a bigger impact on people than you ever imagined. You are going to be more financially successful than you ever imagined and you are going pursue a career that will be more fulfilling than you ever imagined. Trust me. It's going to happen Walter. God has His hand all over you." I knew there was good reason to believe what Matt was saying because after everything he had been through, he remained incredibly resilient. To this day when I talk to Matt and ask him how things are going, he always responds, "Fantastic Walter! Things are going great." It wasn't that Matt lived in la-la land or that he stuck his head in the sand. He knew exactly what was going on, but Matt always believed that "this too shall pass" and that good things were ahead to those who wait.

This attitude of optimism is one of the key traits of really successful people. Successful people believe the future holds good things for them regardless of their present circumstances.

> "Successful people believe the future holds good things for them regardless of their present circumstances."

They truly believe that they are going to be okay. They believe that their marriage can still be incredible, and even if it isn't, they are going to be okay. They believe great things for their kids even when they are making terrible decisions. But even if things don't turn out the way they had hoped, they remain positive, believing something good will result. Whether it's the entrepreneur, the CEO or the mother of three children, all who are optimists at heart sincerely believe that tomorrow could be the greatest day of their lives.

Some people hear such talk and accuse optimists of being in a state of denial. Naysayers believe that positive thinking is a set up for failure and disappointment. They think it's better to be a realist than to make up an idealized story about the future to make themselves feel better. Sadly, what the supposed "realist" does not understand is that the attitude we carry today shapes our experience of tomorrow.

> "The attitude we carry today shapes our experience of tomorrow."

In other words, if I expect more disappointment and pain tomorrow, chances are that I will get what I anticipate. However, if my mental attitude is such that I truly believe tomorrow will be a good day, the probability of my experiencing a good day is much, much higher. That's because the experience of a good or bad day is just as much about my outlook as it is about my daily experiences.

I remember reading the story of an 80-year-old man who was being admitted into an assisted living facility by his children. As they were telling him about his new home, the amenities, and the great care he would get there, he said, "Oh yes, I love it. It's a wonderful place. I am so happy there." His children, thinking he was confused, said, "Dad, actually you haven't been there, so you can't say you love it yet -- even though we think you will." Their father's response was filled with enormous amounts of wisdom for successful living. He said, "Oh, I don't have to see it. I've already decided how much I love it." Isn't that great? This man learned that there are some things you simply choose to have a great attitude about. In fact, I am sure that when this wonderful man arrived at the facility, his predetermined attitude allowed him to enjoy his new place of residence even more. Imagine if he had complained and worried and expected things to be uncomfortable. Likely, his experience would be very different. That's the beauty of the optimistic spirit.

Positive people are the ones we enjoy being around the most. I'm not talking about the over-the-top person who comes across as insincere. I'm talking about that friend, coworker, spouse or boss who is consistently encouraged and leaves a trail of hope wherever they go. Those are the people we love to be around and support. We grow weary of negative people. It's one thing for us to honestly share the challenges in our lives with people. All of us have bouts of pain and disappointment. But that is very different from the person who is a chronic complainer. You ask how their work is going and they tell you how swamped they are, or how horrible their boss is or how tired they are of working with incompetent people. You ask someone how they are doing personally and they say things like, "Any day above the ground is a good day for me." Or how about the person who always talks about their ailments? Their back is killing them, they feel tired all the time, they feel stressed out, and on and on. We could continue with examples, but you get the point. How refreshing it is to spend time with someone who can share honestly what is going on in their life but who retains a belief that things are good -- and will get better. All of us have worked with and for people who have embraced both approaches to life. It's not difficult to choose who you prefer to be around.

I worked for Danny when I was in college and boy was he a downer. He came down hard on us when things weren't going well. He rarely smiled. I don't remember a single instance of receiving a compliment from him and he acted as if work was a burden. He was my manager for two years and it was draining. After he left, Mr. Earl replaced him. Talk about night and day. Mr. Earl was a large man who loved to laugh big and loud. He asked us how we were doing every day when we arrived at work. On several occasions, Mr. Earl called me into his office just to visit for a few minutes and ask how college was going, how I was enjoying my job and if there was anything I needed at work. You can bet that my attitude was different than it was under my old boss. I approached work with a renewed energy and sense of purpose. I was a better employee under his management. Mr. Earl loved his job and he loved working with people. He was a great example of optimism and the impact of an optimistic attitude on the people around you.

When I made my list of all the successful people in my life, I was stunned to see how the overwhelming majority of them were all such positive people. Great parents are positive parents. Great marriages thrive on positive energy. Great corporate cultures are great because of the positive vibe that people feel when they work there. Great artists and athletes and writers all have a deep belief within their craft that they have the ability to achieve their goals and dreams. That is what drives them.

Have you ever met someone who was forced to confront a challenge so potentially life-shattering that your small complaints were immediately put into perspective? Nick Vujicic had that effect on me. Nick was born without arms or legs. I saw him one day in a Starbucks, buzzing around in his BMW wheelchair with a big smile and positive energy that was contagious. I immediately got on my computer to look up his story. It's quite a tale.

Nick was a person who had every right to be bitter and depressed. He did face a terrible time of hopelessness and struggle when he was younger. But he came through with a determination not just to live normally but to live better than anyone could have imagined. Not only does he refuse to be defined by his physical constraints, but he travels the world, speaking to tens of thousands and sharing a message of optimism, resilience and faith. Nick, far more than anyone else, has shown me the power of optimism and how far a resilient spirit can take a person in life.

As we move into the exercise section of this chapter, I want you to be honest with yourself and see where you fall on the optimism scale. The great thing about optimism is that it can improve immediately because it is a choice. We get to decide what this looks like in our lives. So take a look at the exercises below and allow yourself to be challenged to grow further in your optimistic attitude.

Remember, optimism is not sticking your head in the sand and ignoring reality. Rather it is being aware of what reality is and then choosing to believe that things can and will get better. This is the attitude of great people. This is the attitude of triumph. I can think of few great accomplishments from habitually negative people.

> “True success is driven by the spirit that believes in what is still possible, regardless of what has already occurred.”

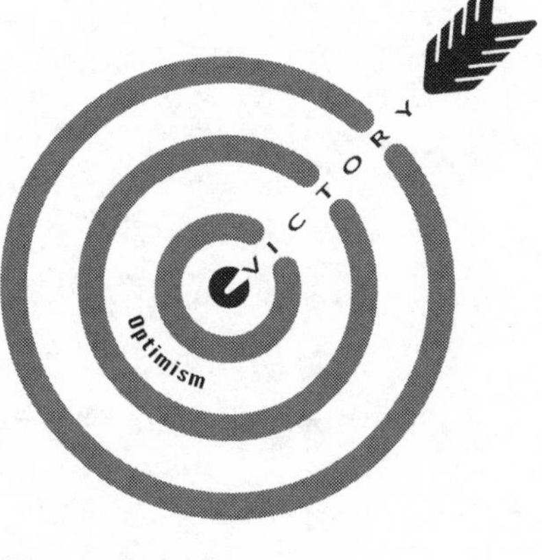

KEY POINTS

- Optimism is not denying reality. Optimism is being aware of reality yet truly believing that things can and will get better.
- No one wants to be around negative people.
- Positive people are more resilient when it comes to experiencing setbacks and failures.
- Optimism is a choice that each of us makes.

APPLICATION EXERCISES

1. Self-Awareness Exercise: over the next three days, try to be aware of yourself doing two things:

   a. Did you complain or criticize anything? If so, how many times did you catch yourself? (Write it down to help you remember)

   ____

   ____

   ____

   ____

   ____

   b. Did you speak positively and with encouragement to anyone? If so, how many times did you find yourself doing this? (Write it down to help you remember)

   ____

   ____

   ____

   ____

2. Accountability Exercise: Ask a few people who have regular access to you on a daily basis to help you be more aware of the presence of complaining or criticizing in your life. Whenever they hear you start complaining, you need them to stop you right away and say, "Are you complaining?" or "Are you criticizing?"

3. Feedback Exercise: Type the following on a sheet of paper: "In an effort this year to continue improving, I want to grow in the area of being encouraging and more positive with those around me. On a scale of 1-10, please write where you would place me on this scale with 1 being low and 10 being high. Also, please add any comments that you think would be helpful. I am asking you because I consider you someone who will be honest. When you are done, just put the sheet back in the envelope and return it to me."

Note: Most people on a 1-10 scale will give others a "7" as a positive safe score. A "7" means you are doing fine in their book but everyone can improve. You are looking for an 8-10 score which is a strong validation of people perceiving you as a positive and encouraging person.

D R E A M W A L L

Anything goes on this page. White page brainstorming and idea creation can be very powerful—write anything that comes to mind or anything you have read that triggers your thoughts about OPTIMISM. Don't leave this page blank!

RELATIONAL SKILLS

"The ability to deal with people is as purchasable a commodity as sugar or coffee and I will pay more for that ability than for any under the sun."

- John D. Rockefeller

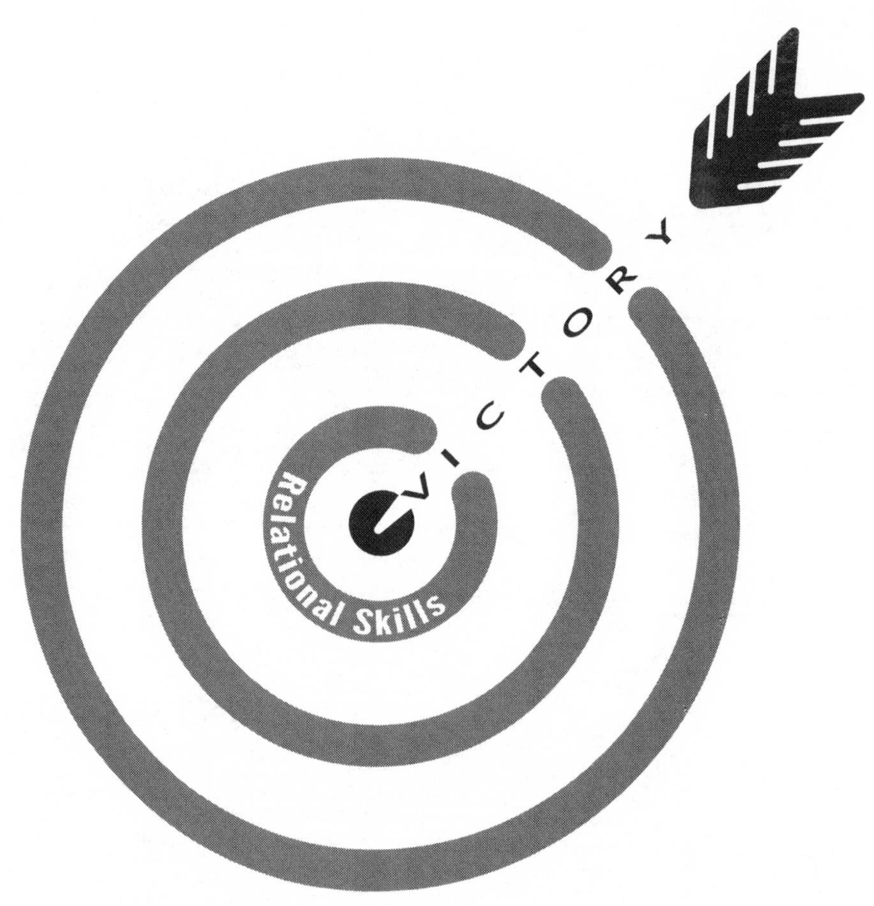

SIX

RELATIONAL SKILLS: THE BUILDING BLOCKS OF A SUCCESSFUL LIFE

Think of the person (or people) in your life who you just absolutely love to be around. Who are they? Of all the people you know, why do *these* particular people come to mind? Why are *they* the ones that you enjoy the most? I would venture to guess the reason you look forward to being with them is because they connect with you in ways that others do not. There is something about the time you spend together and the conversations that occur that seems effortless. It doesn't take a lot of work. It just flows. The ability to relate to people with different personality types and from different backgrounds is one of the distinguishing traits of people who achieve great success in life. In essence, they have learned the powerful skill of knowing how to *connect* with people.

A study was conducted by an Ivy League university that focused on their largest alumni donors. The university wanted to see if there were common traits among successful alumni that were evident when they were students. Were these high-achievers Phi Beta Kappa honors students? Did they participate in top-level research during their time on campus? Were they the computer and science geniuses who never left their labs? What researchers discovered, to their surprise, was that these wealthy alumni donors were all highly involved in campus social clubs and sports organizations. Many participated and held offices in their clubs, fraternities and sororities, and intramural and collegiate sports. In other words, they showed a healthy balance between their academic and social lives. Being involved in the social dynamics of their collegiate years was just as important to them as performing well in their classes. Clearly, their success should also be attributed to intelligence and hard work. But just as significantly, they excelled because they had the ability to work with a wide variety of people and manage their relationships exceptionally well.

You've met people like this, haven't you? Maybe you had a random encounter with a stranger and you ended up having a great conversation. Maybe there is someone you have known for a long time who just knows how to communicate with you. Whatever the case, when it happens, the time spent together is easy. For the most part, everyone can relate well with some of the people they know. However, there are some people who have learned to do this with virtually everyone they meet. They aren't being fake or disingenuous. They simply know how to adapt themselves to the people they're with and circumstances they encounter. The better a person is at authentically connecting on this relational level, the more effective and successful they will be with everyone around them.

I was recently reminded that even the most pleasant and easygoing people sometimes struggle in this area. David and I had a great friendship and we had a lot of respect for each other. One thing about David however was that he was very reserved. He didn't disclose a lot of personal feelings and wasn't particularly inclined to ask many questions. That didn't matter to me, though. David was smart, incredibly well-read, very kind and a good listener. I knew when he and I got together that I would take the responsibility to steer the conversation and just enjoy the time talking.

David had been married for several years to a wonderful girl and never complained about his marriage. So I always just assumed that his wife had learned to accept him just the way he was, though I knew it must have been challenging at times. One day David surprised me by disclosing that he and his wife were not doing well. In fact, she had been unhappy for a long time. The fact that David shared this with me meant the situation was probably worse than he was communicating. As I probed and listened, the main issue became clear: David's wife felt he didn't really care about her any more. Her conclusion was based on the fact that her husband would never sit down and have conversations with her. The only time he asked questions was when he needed information. She knew this was a part of David's personality and she loved him. But over the years, the lack of communication began to take a toll on her heart. David said that because he and I had been friends for so many years, that maybe I would have some advice for him.

I told him I was honored that he would be so transparent with me and that I would be happy to share some things that I have observed about him over the years. I then spoke very honestly about the relational challenges that I also face when he and I meet. I told him that he scores high in many areas of his life. He's a hard worker, full of integrity, always lends a hand and he provides great security for his family. All that being said, I told him that his biggest liability is his inability to connect with people and drive good, thoughtful conversations. I told him he wouldn't change an ingrained pattern overnight, but I assured him I was confident he could greatly improve in this area if he wanted to and, as a result, possibly create a renewed love with his wife. He said he always wanted to improve in this area but just never knew how.

At that point, I took out a piece of paper and began to write a very simple model, which I will discuss shortly. This model would help David have a plan whenever he interacted with people. Only time will tell what will happen with his marriage, but I do know this: If he hadn't made the decision to improve his relational skills, his marriage would never survive. Not only would his marriage suffer, but David would miss out on many opportunities to connect with other important people in his life not to mention the other life challenges that come from not being a good communicator.

This story highlights the importance of learning the skills to connect *relationally* with people. You will never be a great parent, a great friend or a great business leader unless you know how to communicate with all kinds of people. Anybody with more than one child knows this fact.

> "You can love your children equally, but to truly be effective, you have to learn how to speak to each one *differently*."

Every child has unique needs and expectations. Whether these factors are part of their personality or a result of their circumstances, parents have to be able to recognize these differences and adjust their approach. This is true for friends, for coworkers and for the people you lead in organizations. I can't tell you how many times I have seen people create opportunity for themselves or get a promotion simply because they connected well with others. Do this and opportunities will abound. Choose not to do this and you will face frustrating challenges.

Many years ago when I was going through a particularly difficult time, I asked a friend of mine who was a pastor in Dallas if he could recommend a therapist in the area. He said without a moment's hesitation that there is only one person he would see. He told me his name was Paul and that he had never met anyone with this man's level of insight, intellect and ability to connect with people. I didn't call Paul right away, but a few months later at a going away party for a mutual friend, I met him in the kitchen while we were refilling our plates. What a small world. Paul and I hit it off immediately. He had a unique ability to ask penetrating questions and show sincere interest in what I was saying. It was a great example of natural and effortless conversational flow. Now you don't have to be a professional therapist to have this skill, but you do have to have a sincere desire to listen to others and take the time to engage them.

Over time, Paul and I became close friends. One of the things that continued to impress me was how easily he connected with everyone. He had the ability to shift gears depending on who he was with, which is partly what allowed him to be so effective with such a wide variety of people. Paul's ability to build bridges quickly and establish rapport both professionally and personally made him greatly loved by hundreds of people. These skills that he demonstrated are essential. Whether it's marriage, parenting, friendships, leading a team or driving sales, success in all of these areas requires having strong relational abilities.

So let me show you how you can better build your skills in this area. I have discovered over the years that highly relational people do four things exceptionally well. I like to use the acronym C.A.R.E. because when you see this done well or when you experience it yourself, you get the real sense that relational people honestly do CARE. If you want to greatly improve all of your relationships or if you want to continue to increase your influence in the workplace, then focus on these four things and turn them into habits.

A Model for Relationship Success

First of all, you can't fake it. People can see that from a mile away. So, ironically the first trait in the C.A.R.E. model is the word "***care***." You have to genuinely *care* about those around you. Managers who don't genuinely care about their people will almost exclusively focus on the bottom line at work. But *great* managers do care for their people. They take the time to know what their team members' aspirations are. They know what is generally going on in their lives. They make the time to visit and talk. Organizational leaders who find themselves too busy to do this will miss out on a lot of untapped potential with their team because they are not making the time to connect and build strong bridges of trust.

Likewise, you have to care about having a great marriage and desire to stay deeply connected with your spouse. You have to care about being a great parent who wants to have a great relationship with your children. You have to care about your customers. You have to convince them that their interests are just as important to you as your own. Caring about someone is not about what you can *get* from them. It's about what you can BE for them. It's about what you can do to truly help them if they are in need. It's about taking a real interest in others and making time for them. Examples of this abound in history. Let's consider for a moment an icon of relational compassion--Mother Theresa.

Mother Theresa is so well known and well respected, that her life's work has transformed her name into a descriptive category all by itself. If someone ever described you as a "Mother Theresa," it would be one of the finest compliments you could receive. Mother Theresa gave up everything to serve the poorest of the poor in Calcutta, India. She invested the totality of her life in building relationships with the poor, the sick and the dying as well as the strong, the powerful and influential of this world. Everyone loved and respected her because of the absolute depth of her love for everyone she met.

Think about that for a moment. Mother Theresa's influence cut across all social levels. The weak and vulnerable knew that she was for them. And powerful leaders understood that she was for them as well, because her work would ultimately benefit society as a whole. Because of Mother Theresa's dedication to the world, we equate her name with the essence of love, goodness, and service. This is the power of being *relational*. When people are convinced about how much you care for them, they will go to great lengths to do whatever they can to help you succeed. Though we may never love like Mother Theresa did, we all have within us the powerful ability to show compassion and connect with the people around us.

Unfortunately, too many people find it difficult to show real concern. That's because it takes up your time and it requires emotional capacity. It can sometimes be messy. And it can interfere with other things you would prefer to do. I can promise you this, though. If you take time on a regular basis to care about others, it will come back in spades someday. Obviously you don't practice caring in order to ultimately benefit yourself. But that's the way life works. To the degree that we give, is generally the degree to which we receive back.

The second thing relational people do well is they ***act***. They don't just say that they care. They follow up with whatever support is needed. When I was going through a challenging time, I shared some of the details with someone I knew, but not very well. You would have called him an acquaintance, perhaps, but definitely not a close friend—yet. After my sharing, I was amazed at how quickly he began to follow up with me. He didn't just walk away after the conversation and move on with his own life. He took the time to *act* by calling me, texting me and making time to meet with me over coffee and lunch. He quickly became one of my closest friends, not because he simply cared, but because he acted on what he cared about.

Many people care about others and are well-intentioned. But they never take action. They either get too busy, it slips their mind or they keep reminding themselves that they need to follow up until the passage of time makes it awkward. Unfortunately, this is how life is for far too many of us. But the person who intentionally *acts* on what they care about will find it makes all the difference in the world. How many times have we said to ourselves after talking to someone or hearing about someone's problem that we ought to do something? I know I have, many times. These days when I see a need I try to act on it right away because I know if I don't, it probably won't happen. Listening is great and having a caring heart is wonderful. But you have to act. It's taking action that puts real muscle behind your words and demonstrates real concern for those around you.

The third characteristic of relational people is that they ***remember***. Again, it's great to care and it's great to take action. Those two things alone will separate you from the majority of people. But, if you take the time to remember someone's circumstances and then follow up with that person, you have taken the relationship to another level. Have you ever had someone circle back to ask how you were doing after you told them about some challenges you were going through? This is a lesson I take right out of my wife's playbook. I don't know if it's a female thing, but my wife seems to remember everything people share with her. She doesn't just listen and act, but somehow she remembers and follows up with a phone call or a text message. If she bumps into an acquaintance, she knows their circumstances and immediately asks for an update. My wife's ability to remember is truly remarkable and it's one that I continue to strive to improve.

I remember a particularly humiliating example of failing to remember a personal detail. A friend who I don't see very often was in town to see his mother because his father had just passed away. He and I spoke for about 30 minutes and I shared my condolences. About six months later, I ran into him again and asked how his father was doing. He replied that his father had passed away several months ago, shortly before we saw each other last. I was incredibly embarrassed and immediately recalled our prior meeting. I apologized for my lapse and he was very gracious. My point is that if I had remembered our last conversation and had taken the initiative to show I cared by asking how his family was handling the loss, I could have deepened our relationship instead of being forced to apologize. It's a lesson we sometimes have to learn the hard way, but there are some tools that can help. One of the big advantages we have today is the technology at our fingertips that reminds us of dates, details, deadlines, and appointments. Most phones have reminder apps and electronic calendars. There are also apps for detailed note taking so we have a record of items to review later. In other words, there are fewer excuses today for forgetfulness.

I am convinced that the better we are at remembering important things in people's lives, the greater our relationships will be with everyone around us. Facebook has saved the day for many of us when it comes to remembering birthdays. Prior to birthday announcements automatically popping up, I never knew until it was too late. Again, whether it's remembering a birthday or remembering the passing of someone close to you, the better we are at recalling personal details, the better our relationships will be.

The fourth and final element of effectively connecting with others is learning how to ***engage*** in a conversation. I have joked many times that someday I am going to write a book entitled Two Monologues Don't Equal a Dialogue! I can't tell you how many times I have watched conversations go back and forth with two people hardly ever asking any questions. It's basically two people talking AT each other and never really creating a conversation. They are never engaging each other. They are just piggybacking off each other's statements. It looks something like this:

Person A: *I can't wait for this summer, I am going to the beach for vacation.*

Person B: *No way, me too!*

Person A: *Yeah, I'm going to San Diego.*

Person B: *Cool, I'm going to Destin in Florida.*

Person A: *I've never been to San Diego, but I hear it's awesome.*

Person B: *Yeah, Destin is awesome too. I've been there three times and it's beautiful.*

Person A: *We are going to stay at this really cool hotel where I hear there are a lot of famous guests.*

Person B: *That's how Destin is. I've seen lots of celebrities there before too!*

Person A: *That's cool. Well, it should be a good summer for us then.*

Person B: *Yeah, definitely!*

Many people who just read that interaction might wonder what the problem is with it. On the surface, it looks like a perfectly good exchange between two people. The problem is that both people had multiple opportunities to probe and ask questions. Each person could have gleaned additional information and shown genuine interest in the other. Instead, they just talked about themselves and used each other's statements as a springboard for their own. In effect, this was two monologues disguised as a dialogue. You would be amazed how much self-referential language is used in conversations. Self-referential language is when people use other people's statements to reference something about themselves. It looks like conversation, but it's simply two people talking about themselves and not genuinely taking an interest in each other.

A couple of summers ago, my son Cooper and I drove to pick up his three cousins so we could all go to the mall. My son at the time was 12 and his cousins were three girls ages 12, 13, and 15. They all piled into my car and off we went. As we were driving, they all went on and on about what was going on in their lives, what they thought about the topic of the moment and what they wanted to do that summer. After about 15 minutes, I couldn't take it anymore. I blurted out, "Hey guys, you are killing me! Do you know we have been in the car for almost 15 minutes and you guys haven't asked each other one single question?

All you're doing is talking about yourselves. You need to start learning how to ask questions and take an interest in each other's lives!"

Well, you can imagine the playfully sarcastic questions I started hearing after that. They all began to ask me questions about how I was doing, what was going on with my life and what I was reading. They started teasingly asking each other question after question. To be honest it was really funny. What's great is that they still ask me questions two years later after that car ride. They knew I was right about the importance of taking the time to ask each other questions.

Knowing how to engage people in a conversation is a crucial skill in developing relational skills. If you ask too many questions, it sounds more like an interview. If you don't ask enough questions, then it sounds like it's all about you. There's a healthy balance that all of us need to strive for in order to build stronger relationships with the people around us. It sounds easy but it's not. It takes work but the payoff is great.

One of the tools that I use when I do professional coaching is what I call the ***4Q Rule***. The 4Q Rule says that you cannot leave any conversation without asking at least four questions to the person you are talking to. It may not seem like a big deal, but try it sometime. For some people this may not be that difficult. But for others it's incredibly revealing. I remember doing a coaching session with someone who always talked about himself. I mean always. I never heard so many "I's" in my life over the course of an hour. Finally at the end of our session, I said, "Listen Ryan, I want you to do something for me tomorrow. I want you to use what I call the 4Q Rule. With everyone you talk to tomorrow, I want you to ask them at least four questions before the conversation ends." Ryan didn't understand why I would ask him to do this, but I told him that I would come back at the end of the next day to hear how things went. He agreed.

The next day I went by Ryan's office at 4 p.m. I asked how the 4Q Rule went. This is an exact quote of his reply. "Oh my goodness, that was so hard. It didn't seem like it was that big of a deal, but it was. Why was that so hard for me to do?" Bingo! Perfect. That was exactly what I was hoping for. So with all of the compassion I could muster I said, "Because you are a terrible listener Ryan. Your communication style just goes one way and you have never really worked on taking the time to ask questions and make conversations a two-way street. You have to improve in this area so people feel like they can be a participant in their conversations with you." I wasn't sure how he was going to respond to this, but he said if it hadn't been for the 4Q Rule, he would not have agreed with me. To his credit, he began making the effort to ask questions whenever we met. Breaking old habits isn't easy, but it can definitely be done with awareness and commitment.

So remember, if you want to improve on your relational skills, do a little personal inventory and ask yourself if you take the time to:

Care
Act
Remember
Engage

Do these things and I promise you that every relationship -- with your employees, coworkers, spouse, children and friends -- will greatly improve!

KEY POINTS

- Being relational is about knowing how to build trust and connect with people.
- In order to be relational, you have to C.A.R.E. This involves:

    Caring for others by listening.

    Acting to help people when you become aware of a need.

    Remembering so you can circle back and follow up.

    Engaging people in conversation by asking questions.

APPLICATION EXERCISES

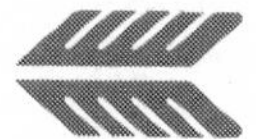

1. Think of the last three or four people who you showed genuine care and concern for. Write their names down and describe specifically how you cared.

____

____

____

____

____

2. If you think you could definitely work on being a better listener, then practice the 4Q Rule with the next few people you interact with. Don't end the conversation until you have asked them at least four questions.

3. Who do you need to follow up with to see how they are doing? Write two or three of their names down and determine how you will follow up with them. Practicing "remembering" is crucial in building deeper relationships.

____

____

____

____

____

____

DREAM WALL

Anything goes on this page. White page brainstorming and idea creation can be very powerful—write anything that comes to mind or anything you have read that triggers your thoughts about RELATIONAL SKILLS. Don't leave this page blank!

YEARNING

WELL, ERIC GOT A PROMOTION.
ANOTHER FELLOW EMPLOYEE MOVES AHEAD WHILE I STAY AT THE SAME LEVEL YEAR AFTER YEAR.
©2014 DAVID WILBORN

YEAH...

MAYBE IF YOU DISPLAYED AMBITION OR INITIATIVE OF SOME SORT.
NAH.

"Improvement begins with 'I.' "

- Arnold H. Glasow

SEVEN

YEARNING:
YOU NEVER ARRIVE UNTIL IT'S OVER!

When I was compiling my list of successful people, it quickly became apparent that one of the core qualities they shared was that they all *yearned* for excellence. They were committed to *continuously improving themselves*. They did not sit back when things were good. They wanted more. They wanted a lot more. The outstanding and successful parents that I know never remain content with their relationships with their children. They work every day to continue to grow and deepen these relationships. Couples in outstanding marriages never take their relationship for granted. Both partners constantly work at making their marriage better because they believe there is always room to keep improving it. Those who are financially successful continually work hard to develop and advance their skills in order to give themselves better opportunities. Complacency does not exist in their vocabulary!

I'm convinced that one of the primary reasons most people give up on their goals is because they do not see results as quickly as they would like. Living in an instant gratification culture makes the daily work of improving much more challenging for many people because the return on their investment often takes quite some time before they see significant results. For example, everyone knows it takes time to get results from exercising. Yet many start going to the gym and eating healthier only to stop within just a few weeks. The reason? They don't see significant results fast enough and they lose their motivation. There is no arguing with the fact that results inspire people and help drive them to keep pressing on. However, I can think of very few worthwhile things in life that don't require a period of sustained work in order to gain real lasting benefits. Sure there are times when results are instant. But many gains are quickly lost if a person doesn't maintain the discipline to stick with their routine or plan.

People can lose 5 or 10 pounds in a week and feel inspired. But once they plateau, what often happens? After the easy pounds come off, their motivation begins to dwindle. Many who start on a weight loss plan ultimately slide back to their original weight -- and maybe even gain a few pounds. Or maybe the student who decided she was going to really buckle down and study that semester was still making poor grades after a couple of weeks of determined effort. What does she do? She goes back to her former, undisciplined habits because she did not see results soon enough. Rather than recognizing that study habits take months and even years to develop, she loses her motivation and resorts to what is habitual and familiar and consequently reinforces to herself the lie that she's not very smart.

When I was 15, my father sat my brother and me down to talk about financial security and retirement. He pulled out a graph that showed us the power of compounding interest over a 45-year period. He said, "Guys listen, if you put $2,000 a year away into an IRA for just seven years and never touch it again, you will end up with over $1 million by the time you turn 60! In other words, once you turn 22 or 23, you don't have to touch your account ever again, and when you retire, you will have a very large sum of money waiting for you." Well, my older brother, being the wise and dutiful one, couldn't believe it. His eyes lit up and he couldn't wait to start. My dad even said that he would match us dollar-for-dollar so that we only had to save $1,000 a year. We both had jobs and mom and dad paid for everything, so it should not have been a problem for either of us to do this. My brother got right on it and has never missed a year. When I turned 22, however, I didn't have a single dime put away! The reason was simple: I couldn't spend the money *right now* and it took "*too long*" for it to grow. I remember thinking, "45 years from now? What can I possibly do with that much money when I am that old?" Now that I'm in my mid-40s, I laugh when I think about that story. The answer today to my youthful self is, of course, *a lot*.

Whether it's investing in learning, relationships or in savings and retirement, wanting instant results is the primary reason why people don't stick with commitments. If the results aren't immediate and they can't enjoy the fruit of their work *now*, they would rather spend their time and money today. What a terribly short-sighted view to have in life. It is well researched that people who read gain knowledge that gives them an advantage over those who rarely open a book. So why don't more people read good substantive material every day? For many, it's because there is no immediate benefit derived from reading a particular book. They could spend that time tackling their to-do list or they could read entertaining and leisurely material instead. I am convinced that the inability to see the long-term benefits that come from present day efforts is one of the major reasons people don't stick with good habits even when they know that it will give them tremendous advantages over those who don't.

What if you were told that if you read 10 books this year and passed an exam after each book, you would receive $1 million at the end of the year? Do you think you would make the time to read every day? I venture to say there is little doubt about it. You might even take notes to make sure you comprehended and retained what you were reading. I know I would. The reason is obvious: the return on your investment is in sight. What if you were guaranteed to lose any amount of weight you wanted in the next six months if you simply exercised for 30 minutes a day for four days of the week? There would be no plateaus, just continuous weight loss every week when you get on the scale. Would this encourage more people to stick with their exercise program for those six months? There is little doubt about it. Most people would stick with the plan because they would be motivated by successful weight loss every week. Unfortunately, life doesn't work this way. Life is rigged. We reap what we sow, both in rewards and negative consequences. However, life will provide us what we ask of it if we are willing to do the work it requires. For real accomplishment to occur, you must have sustained effort. It's this attitude of "yearning" for more that drives such success. It's the daily pursuit of continual improvement that, over time, will always pay you in amounts equal to or greater than what you put in.

For example, let's say you really want to grow your business. If this is your goal, you will have to ask yourself some very honest questions:

1. What is your plan? Have you spent time writing it out?

2. Are you executing your plan every day of every week of every month to drive your business forward?

3. What are you doing to position yourself as a subject matter expert in your field?

4. What are you doing to get greater exposure for your business? Be specific.

5. Have you been spending regular time learning new strategies for growing your business? How savvy are you with social media? Are you actively reading and learning how to leverage these new platforms to further your company's success? Have you studied the growth strategies of your competitors?

All of these questions and many more have to be answered and taken seriously if you truly want to grow your company. Recently I was doing some research about social media platforms and the reasons for their slow adoption by a large percentage of businesses today. The top two reasons I discovered were 1) Results are not seen quickly enough and 2) Business leaders are so busy doing other things that they don't make the time to learn the technology and the strategies to make these tools work for their company. Sound familiar? How often have these same two reasons hindered us from moving forward?

Dan is a good friend of mine. Since I met him in high school, he has always been a big "idea guy." He is always into something new. He is the type of person who shows deep interest and passion about something right out of the gate. Initially, his enthusiasm for the project is incredibly contagious. You feel like you want to drop what you're doing and -- based on his level of excitement alone -- join his efforts. The problem I have observed with Dan is that he eventually loses interest when the real work arrives. I can't tell you how many times he told me he was starting to learn Spanish because he knew that would be a valuable skill. I always agreed with him. People who know Spanish have an employment advantage over people who don't, particularly in certain parts of the country. Time and again, he would get started on a new audio or video series or with a new introduction to Spanish book, but within a few weeks he was on to something new. The idea of knowing Spanish was exciting, but the real work to acquire the skill was far less appealing. It was the same thing with making money for Dan. He wanted to get rich quick so he jumped on board with many multi-marketing companies because he was convinced how easily their products would sell. Unfortunately, he quit them all when he realized how much hard work was actually required.

In the beginning, learning something new can be fast-paced and exciting. But students in any discipline eventually hit a point where the novelty wears off and the process feels more like hard work and repetition. This is the point where Dan would always stop. This is the point where most people stop. Whether it's learning Spanish, gaining social media skills, studying finance and accounting to improve your business, meeting new people, stretching your social and interpersonal skills or any number of other beneficial practices, when the shiny new luster wears off and challenges begin to appear like more of a pain than an adventure, this is where most people quit. But this is where there is good news. This is the point at which you have the real opportunity to shine. To stand above the crowd. To add to your "success tool belt." If you continue on while most others quit, it will just be a matter of time before you see extraordinary results from your dedication.

The key to success is having the willingness to accept that the return on your investment each day may *seem* negligible. When people want results more than they are willing to commit long term to a process, they struggle to stick with things that only pay out after an investment of time. All the advertisements that seem too good to be true by promising amazing results in 30 days are often just that—too good to be true. Lose 30 pounds in 30 days? Maybe. But keep it off without any additional effort thereafter? It's unlikely. Take this seminar and change your life? Read this book and become financially independent? Sure. On and on it goes. Lots of promises prey on our weaker nature. People that fall for this stuff are looking for the path of least resistance. The path that pays the greatest reward takes guts, grit and yearning. It's work. It's every day. It's a commitment to continue even when I stop seeing the benefits in front of me because I know if I put the time and effort in consistently, life will pay what I ask of it. So what is it that drives a person to want to endure the painstaking process of achieving excellence? Simply put, it is that they have a mindset that yearns for more and that is willing to pay whatever the price is to achieve their vision. Sometimes that price requires lifelong determination. For instance, consider the amazing story of Nola Ochs.

It's been said, "You're never too old to learn" which is why I can't think of a better example of someone who proves that adage than Nola. This determined woman owns the distinction of being the oldest person to graduate from college as well as the oldest person to get a master's degree.

Nola was born in 1911 and took her first college course at Fort Hays State University (then called Kansas State College) in 1930. But her studies were interrupted by raising four children and working on the family farm. When Nola's husband passed away after 39 years of marriage, she returned to school, this time at Dodge City Community College. With only 30 hours left to complete her undergraduate degree, Nola returned to Fort Hays, moved into a student apartment and finished what she started. She received her bachelor's degree in 2007 at 95 years of age and was honored as Kansas Woman Leader of the Year! Nola then went on to complete her master's degree in 2010 – at 98 years of age. That's what happens when you *yearn* for more in your life!

So let's get specific. What do you yearn for? What thing(s) do you find yourself longing for with a deep passion? What are you willing to work incredibly hard for that will require an enormous dedication from you? Yearning for something without the required commitment to do whatever is necessary to achieve it makes it nothing more than a mere wish. The distance between wishing and yearning is miles apart. Everybody wishes: "I wish I had a master's degree." "I wish I weighed less." "I wish I didn't have so much chronic pain." "I wish I had more money." "I wish I had better relationships with people." "I wish my boss would notice me more." "I wish my marriage was better." "I wish I could spend more time with my kids." This list could go on and on describing all kinds of things most people wish for. Everybody wishes, but only a few truly yearn. This is the difference between people who experience real "victory" in their lives versus people who are still waiting for their ship to come in. Here's the thing -- your ship is not going to come in. You have to make your own ship and then get out on the sea and go after whatever it is you long for. One of my favorite quotes that challenges me every time that I think of it says:

> "In order to discover new lands, one must consent to lose sight of the shore for a very long time."
>
> *- Andre Gide*

This is so true. Losing sight of the shore is the precondition to discovering new lands that are worth discovering. We must be willing to let go of what is easy. We can't continue to live in the realm of what's comfortable. Losing sight of the shore means stretching ourselves toward what can sometimes be fearful and uncertain. It could even require giving up something that is very hard to let go of.

I have a friend who has wanted to give up smoking for years. She always wished she could quit, but she ultimately failed each time she tried. One day she made a decision to quit again, but it seemed that something was different this time. Circumstances had occurred in her life that challenged her to become a stronger person in several areas. As of this writing, it has been more than three months since she has picked up a cigarette. She had to give something up in order to achieve what she was yearning for. She is yearning for control over her life. She no longer wants to allow people and things to dictate her behavior. I don't know what my friend's future holds, but I do know that right now she is harnessing the power of yearning and it is making a huge difference in her life.

What about you? Think about the things you wish for. Which of those things would you love to yearn for? Which of those things are you willing to pay the big price for? I love the tagline of financial advisor Dave Ramsey when he says, "Live like no one else so that someday you can live like no one else." That's exactly what we are talking about. To live like no one else is to do the things that no one else is doing so that someday the benefits will allow you to live better than the great majority of other people. This is the heart of what yearning is all about.

Think about Michael Jordan, Tiger Woods, Roger Federer or any other high achiever in sports. All of these people lived like no one else to get to where they did. This principle of yearning applies to every area of our lives. To have an exceptional marriage, to be an exceptional parent, to be an exceptional leader, to be an exceptional person in any key area of life requires the same level of commitment to the daily grind of small things that eventually will yield incredible returns. You have to be willing to accept the long, and sometimes boring, drive down a Midwest highway in order to get to the beauty of the coast. Nothing worthwhile ever comes easy. In the same way, few things in life that are really worthwhile will be exciting to prepare for all the time. Preparation takes a lot of work, a lot of repetition and an enormous amount of dedication. One of my close friends whose name is Christopher is without a doubt one of the best tennis coaches in the country. I remember him saying one day at a clinic, "If this doesn't get boring, then you haven't done it long enough! Being a champion requires long boring roads of intense repetition." What a profound statement about what it takes to achieve excellence. Although the daily grind may not feel very enjoyable along the way, what will make it all worthwhile is the successful end result that follows from all of the hard work you put in.

Nick is a 16-year-old young man who recently demonstrated this to be true. Two years ago, he picked up his dad's guitar and just started strumming and playing around with the instrument. Not long after, he decided he wanted to learn some chords, so he began to ask his dad to show him a few. He began watching instructional videos on YouTube and other clips of great guitarists. Do you know how often he would do this? Every day. He would be the first to tell you that he didn't see huge improvements in his guitar playing right away. It took time, patience and commitment—in other words, yearning to be really good someday. I know this because Nick is my amazing step-son. It seemed everyday I would come home and I would hear Nick playing his guitar and watching videos. He was consumed with it.

Well, the hard work paid off. Two years later, he has been asked on several occasions to lead his youth group of 150+ students in worship on Sunday mornings. What an honor to do that. Some may say "Wow, that is amazing in just two years!" Well, yes, it sure is amazing. But considering the daily investment and commitment Nick put in we should not be surprised. It was just a matter of time. That is the power of yearning for something. It drives you to spend your time every day working towards a goal that isn't just a hope or a wish, but rather is a deep desire to achieve something that you desperately want. So how about you? What do you yearn for? Write down what you yearn for and begin the work of creating a plan. Remember earlier when we discussed the critical role that taking "initiative" plays in success? Yearning without initiative is nothing more than dreaming. So decide today what it is that you really want and let's go after it.

KEY POINTS

- Yearning is all about a commitment to "continuous improvement."
- The results of yearning often take lots of time.
- People give up mainly because they do not see results soon enough.
- The difference between a wish and yearning is the level of commitment one has to achieve the goal in mind.
- Yearning begins with a simple decision followed by a commitment.

APPLICATION EXERCISES

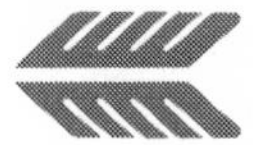

1. Take a sheet of paper and write down five things you WISH for that you have not achieved yet.

2. Now take each of those things you listed and write down what the reason(s) are for your not achieving it yet.

3. Now look at each of the reasons you gave and ask this very important question: Is the reason you gave truly an obstacle that cannot be overcome? If it can be overcome, what would it take?

4. Finally, what do you want to *yearn* for that has only been a wish up until this point? Write it down. Now decide what it will take every day for you to be able to achieve it.

DREAM WALL

Anything goes on this page. White page brainstorming and idea creation can be very powerful—write anything that comes to mind or anything you have read that triggers your thoughts about YEARNING. Don't leave this page blank!

"In reading the lives of great men,
I found that the first victory they won
was over themselves."

- Harry S. Truman

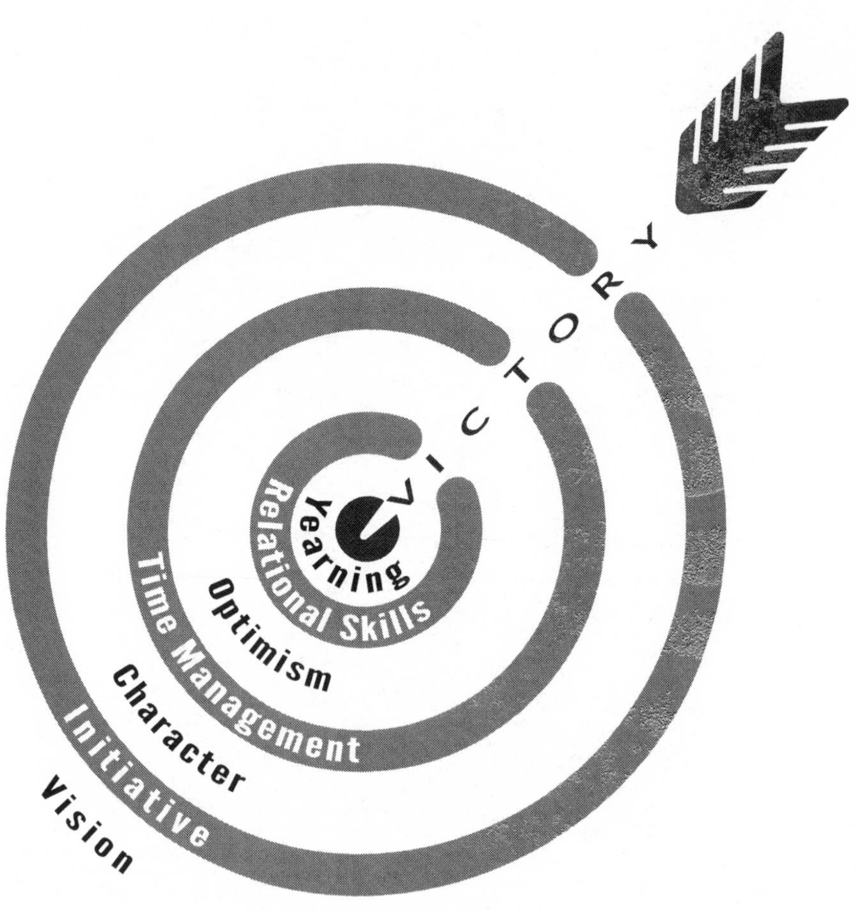

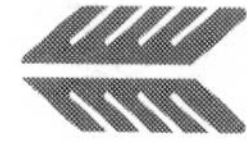

EIGHT

A QUICK REVIEW: PUTTING IT ALL TOGETHER

There is no substitute for repetition, so let's do a quick review of what we have learned. My hope is that you will take the acronym VICTORY, memorize it and begin to apply it to all the important areas of your life. There is power in each of these seven traits. You cannot afford to sacrifice any of them without paying a price. So do yourself a big favor and remember these. Use them at work. Use them in your marriage. Use them in your parenting. Use them in your personal relationships. You will be amazed at the return when you invest in each of these critical elements of success. So let's review:

Vision: a specific and constantly recurring image that instills passion and drives your commitment to achieve it

Initiative: the ability to take action and execute on the important things of your life (usually tied to your vision)

Character: the strength to do what is right when the easier option is available

Time Management: minimizing waste; focusing on your highest priorities

Optimism: resilience; finding opportunity within every difficulty

Relational skills: connecting interpersonally and building trust with others

Yearning: the constant desire for continuous improvement; the "fire in the belly"

Before I started writing this book, I wrote the names of as many people as I could think of who applied these critical traits of success to their lives. As I have gone back over the names on that list, I am even more convinced that anyone who seriously decides to develop and apply the VICTORY model to their lives will see remarkable results. It does not matter what area of your life you decide to focus on.

Remember, you have to begin with a clear ***vision*** of what you want. Block out some time for yourself and think specifically about what you want the key areas of your life to look like. Write your vision down and keep it with you until you have burned the images into your mind. Spend time every day reflecting on these images. Use the exercises at the end of the chapter on vision to help you with this process. Remember, what the mind is filled with will be what it focuses on (and helps you to achieve subconsciously). Let your mind work for you even when you aren't directly thinking about what you want.

Now you are ready to take ***initiative***. Don't forget, vision without initiative is nothing but a hope or a wish. You have to know your plan and then take action. I can't count how many times I have heard people share ideas that ought to be pursued but never see the light of day. You have to decide what you want and then you have to take action and execute! Don't forget to write your plan down and work the plan every day. Nothing great comes easy. So dig down and make yourself act.

You are the only one in control of what you decide to act on. There are excuses for everything. Being too tired, having too much work or not having enough resources such as money or help are common killers of initiative. One thing I have found over the years is that those excuses rarely go away. And if they do, there are new ones to take their place. Know your vision, decide the plan and then take initiative.

If you choose to live a life that regularly seeks the path of least resistance, you will get the results that a life of least resistance produces. People of ***character*** regularly choose the harder path when the easier choice is available. They have learned to avoid the temptation of immediate gratification. Sleeping in is the easier road. Watching television is the easier road. Internet surfing is the easier road. Eating junk food is the easier road. Deciding to start tomorrow is the easier road. Not reading is the easier road. Staying angry is the easier road. There are literally thousands of easier paths to take, but the person of character is willing and able to go down the harder road because rewards come to those who are willing to work. What are your easier roads that tempt you? One thing is for sure. The path of least resistance rarely, if ever, ends at success.

Successful people ***manage their time*** better than everyone else. Being busy is not the same as being productive. Being productive means that you are moving the ball towards the goal line. It's easy to let that phone call distract you from time spent with your child. It's easy to not be fully present with someone when you are tired. It's easy to let secondary issues such as cleaning out your e-mails or straightening your office get in the way of time-sensitive deadlines. In order to make sure you don't live a frantic life, you need to make sure you are diligently protecting yourself from distractions. Developing the ability to say "no" is critical to staying on course. It's not that you shouldn't be willing to help others. But when you are in the middle of one of your high-priority items, you have to be able to say "no." Sometimes this means saying "no" to yourself when you would rather do something else. It's easy for many of us to be lazy and procrastinate. Learn to say "no" to yourself. It's the only way you will ever truly achieve the goals you want so badly. You won't see results right away. But remember that time is your ally. Doing small actions every day over a few years will yield enormous results. Bad habits over time will yield the same thing, except the results will not be good. That is what leads to a life of regret. So clarify your vision, make a plan and take initiative. Choose to do the hard things when necessary and spend your time on what's important.

Achieving anything worthwhile is not going to be easy. In fact there will be times when life seems unbearably challenging if not downright impossible. Obstacles and setbacks are inevitable. It is a universal truth that we will face resistance to anything meaningful that we try to achieve. Examples are numerous. Financial hardships, broken relationships, physical and psychological illnesses and injustice impact all of us in one way or another. It's not about removing these challenges as much as it is about displaying an attitude of not giving up. People who have the ability to maintain a positive mindset in the face of hardships are called ***optimists***. This is one of the key ingredients to achieving great things in life. Believing that "this too shall pass" or that "this is just a necessary step on my path to success" is the attitude we need to help carry us through the bumps and roadblocks of life. Being resilient and having the ability to bounce back is what the optimist practices throughout life. Optimists recover from setbacks and persevere because they truly believe that greater things are possible. They don't give up no matter what stands in their way.

Remember that ***relationships*** are the DNA of life. People who are effective at building strong trustworthy relationships have a major advantage over those who don't. Whether it's in a business setting or personal, learning to build trust with those around you is an essential ingredient for success. Like it or not, people need people to succeed. Those whom we like and trust are the ones we want to see succeed. That's because they connect with us in ways that others do not. The key to building relationships comes down to demonstrating to people that you are "for them." You speak well of them. You encourage them. You listen to them and take the time to understand what's going on in their life. You offer support to them when you can. You express thankfulness and appreciation to them. All of these things help to build strong relationships no matter what the setting is. Whether you are relating to your boss, your employees, your clients, your spouse or your children, these actions demonstrate that you are for them. This commitment to serve the best interests of others is one of the essential elements to your success.

There's an old saying that goes, "you can't steer a parked car." In the VICTORY model, ***yearning*** fuels the forward motion necessary to reach your goals. Yearning is the desire to continually improve oneself. When you find yourself not yearning any more, you will fall into complacency and the negative elements of life will begin to outweigh the positive. All great athletes yearn to be better, which is why they put themselves through rigorous training. All leaders yearn to be even better, which is why they are constantly reading, practicing self-reflection and influencing the people around them toward a particular goal. People who want to improve their financial status are constantly working to increase their opportunities. Some go back to school and finish college. Others may go on to pursue an advanced degree or technical training to learn a new skill. Whatever the case, it is the trait of yearning that drives their continual push forward. I can't think of a single area in life where yearning is not essential to achieving outstanding results. Yearning is the fire in our belly. It is the emotion and passion that comes from yearning that drives us to keep pressing on and to keep setting the bar higher for ourselves so that we can achieve all that we are capable of.

Well there you go. These are the seven traits that you need in your toolkit for life. The great thing is that everyone can develop them further. It will take some work. But few things in life worth achieving come easy. I am excited about the potential that you have to achieve VICTORY in whatever you decide to dedicate yourself towards. Remember, the great thing about success is that it's not just for the gifted and talented. Everyone has the same opportunity. You don't have to be Leonardo Da Vinci or Benjamin Franklin to achieve significant success in your life. You just have to be intentional with one of the greatest gifts all of us are given—time. It's a limited commodity that gets spent every day. Every bit of time that we waste is time we will never get back. But today is a new day. Don't dwell on regrets. Time spent in regret of squandered opportunity is still wasted time! What matters most is working with what you have today.

Have you ever walked a dark path through the woods carrying a flashlight? Flashlights brighten the trail a few feet in front of you, but eventually the light disperses. It's impossible to plan a long distance route with a flashlight. Sure, its tiny beam will help you avoid immediate obstacles so you don't bump into a rock or plant your foot in a stream. But you would never use a flashlight to set a 10-mile course to your destination.

Unlike flashlights, which project light in multiple wavelengths, lasers consist of a single wavelength. Laser beams travel great distances with great power. In other words, a flashlight can brighten your immediate surroundings. But lasers can cross miles and even burn through steel. A hiker with a laser beam could pierce the darkness across several miles *and* probably blast through some of the obstacles on his path! That is the difference a focused life can make. So which are you? Are you more like a flashlight or are you more like a laser beam? Do you just focus on the small distance ahead because you are distracted by too many things? Or are you more like a laser beam with a powerful singular focus?

When we function as a flashlight, we can respond to current circumstances. But we may struggle to make forward progress. In fact, there are stories of hikers who lost their way at night and walked in circles for miles until daylight illuminated the path back home. When our lives are focused like a laser beam, our energies and efforts are no longer scattered. They align to become a powerful force for overcoming adversity, staying on course and reaching our destination.

The wonderful thing about life is that for all practical purposes you are able to map out your own path and begin taking the necessary steps to reach your goals. No doubt there will be times when life will throw something unexpected your way. You will be forced to change course or possibly delay your advancement for a little while. But that is not the same as allowing circumstances to define your path. I have seen far too many people who have allowed setbacks in life to sideline them -- permanently. Divorces, the death of loved ones, moral failures, bankruptcies and other traumatic events can stop you in your tracks. But you cannot let the setbacks and pain of life keep you from forging ahead. This is where an optimistic and resilient spirit helps you get back up and take another step forward.

It's inspiring to hear the stories of people who have overcome major obstacles to achieve absolutely incredible things. I think of people like my friend Stephanie who was diagnosed with a serious form of brain cancer with a very low survival rate. With medicine, perseverance and a positive attitude, she beat it, went on to complete her Ph.D. and now teaches at a university. If that weren't enough, today Stephanie is training for an Ironman race. Talk about optimism and resilience!

Do you want to be a more effective leader at work? Do you want a meaningful and fulfilling career that you love investing in? Do you want a better and more connected marriage? Then learn these principles and commit to your plan. It's not going to just happen. It's going to take a commitment to each of these principles. Whether it's having a better relationship with your kids, improving your health or achieving greater financial stability, the seven traits of VICTORY will help you realize your ultimate goals. You have the tools. You have the knowledge. Now you have to decide what you really want and then go for it. In the immortal words of Apollo Creed to Rocky when he was training him in Rocky III, "There IS NO tomorrow!" There really isn't. Not to the person who yearns for great things. Today is the day.

EXERCISES

SELF ASSESSMENT

1. On a 1-10 scale, how clear are you on the vision of your organization? Circle your answer.

   1 2 3 4 5 6 7 8 9 10

2. Briefly write down what you believe the vision of your organization is:

   ____

   ____

   ____

   ____

3. On a 1-10 scale, how clear is your vision for your professional life? Your personal life? Circle your answer.

   1 2 3 4 5 6 7 8 9 10 *Professional*

   1 2 3 4 5 6 7 8 9 10 *Personal*

4. On a 1-10 scale, rate the following statements:

   I can see with great detail what I want in my professional life.

   1 2 3 4 5 6 7 8 9 10

   I can see with great detail what I want in my relationships.
   1 2 3 4 5 6 7 8 9 10

I feel compelled every day to work towards a specific vision.

1 2 3 4 5 6 7 8 9 10

I find myself talking regularly to people about what I want in my life.

1 2 3 4 5 6 7 8 9 10

5. What is your vision for your professional life?

____

____

____

____

____

____

____

6. Describe your vision for your personal life:

____

____

____

____

____

____

____

____

____

7. On a 1-10 scale, how would you rate yourself as someone who takes initiative? Circle your answer.

1 2 3 4 5 6 7 8 9 10

8. Give three examples of your taking initiative in the past 30 days:

1. ______________________________

____

____

2. ______________________________

____

____

3. ______________________________

____

____

9. What is your vision for your professional life?

____

____

____

____

10. On a 1-10 scale, rate the following statements:

I never have to be reminded to get things done.

1 2 3 4 5 6 7 8 9 10

I never leave things unfinished. I always finish what I start.

1 2 3 4 5 6 7 8 9 10

I am an excellent planner.

1 2 3 4 5 6 7 8 9 10

I never procrastinate.

1 2 3 4 5 6 7 8 9 10

11. What is the next thing you will take initiative in doing?

____

____

____

____

12. Who is the next person you need to take initiative with?

____

13. On a 1-10 scale, rate yourself on the following statements:

I am known for being a person of high integrity.

1 2 3 4 5 6 7 8 9 10

I always do what I say I am going to do.

1 2 3 4 5 6 7 8 9 10

I always share honestly with people when I have an issue with them.

1 2 3 4 5 6 7 8 9 10

I regularly challenge myself to do whatever it takes to be excellent.

1 2 3 4 5 6 7 8 9 10

14. Would you consider yourself someone that forgives easily or holds grudges?

___

15. In what ways do you stretch yourself to grow in your character?

1. ___

___

___

___

2. ___

___

___

___

3. ___

___

___

___

16. On a 1-10 scale, how well would you say you effectively manage your time?

1 2 3 4 5 6 7 8 9 10

17. List your top 5 priorities at work:

1. ______________________________

____

2. ______________________________

____

3. ______________________________

____

4. ______________________________

____

5. ______________________________

____

18. List your top 5 priorities in your personal life:

1. ______________________________

____

2. ______________________________

____

3. ______________________________

____

4. ______________________________

____

5. ______________________________

____

19. Beside each of the above listed priorities, give yourself a letter grade on how well you think you are fulfilling each of them:

A+ A A- B+ B B- C+ C C- D+ D D- F

20. Look at which items you gave lower than a B+ and ask yourself what you will need to do to improve your effectiveness in that area. Write it out.

____

____

____

____

____

____

____

21. Who is the most optimistic person you know? Give three other characteristics of this person when you think of them.

Person: ________________________________

1. ____________________________________

____

2. ____________________________________

____

3. ____________________________________

____

22. Give three examples from your life where you showed strong resilience.

1. ______________________________

____

____

2. ______________________________

23. What are you currently in the middle of that is challenging your optimism and resilience?

24. On a 1-10 scale, how effectively do you build relationships with people?

1 2 3 4 5 6 7 8 9 10

25. What is your biggest challenge in building strong relationships?

____

____

____

____

____

26. Think of five successes you have had in life. What key people were involved in each of those? List the success and the person's name beside each below:

1. ______________________________

____

____

2. ______________________________

____

____

3. ______________________________

____

____

4. ______________________________

____

____

5. ______________________________

____

____

27. When was the last time you wrote a hand-written note of appreciation to someone? Think of three people you should do that for, write their name below, and make a plan to do it within 24 hours.

1. ______________________________
2. ______________________________
3. ______________________________

28. On a 1-10 scale, how diligently do you continue to challenge yourself to grow and develop?

1 2 3 4 5 6 7 8 9 10

29. List three areas in the past year where you have actively grown and developed yourself further.

1. ______________________________

____

____

2. ______________________________

____

____

3. ______________________________

____

____

30. What are two aspects of your life that you would like to improve or develop better?

1. ______________________________

____

____

2. ______________________________

____

____

31. What would you need to do to begin growing in the areas you listed? Write out an action plan below and make the decision to start!

____

____

HOMEWORK: BONUS EXERCISES

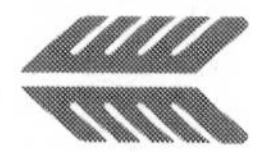

VISION

READ

1. Habit 2: "The 7 Habits of Highly Effective People" by Stephen Covey

2. "Visioneering" by Andy Stanley

ASK

Ask someone who you know is a high achiever the following questions:

1. What does having vision mean to them in their life?

2. What role has vision played in helping them succeed?

3. What advice would they give you about growing your vision?

WRITE

Write a summary of what key takeaways you received from the above readings and questions you asked. Make sure your summary takeaways are written in a way that you can personalize.

INITIATIVE

READ

1. "Execution" by Larry Bossidy & Ram Charan
2. "Execution is the Strategy" by Laura Stack

ASK

Think of a person you know who always seems to "get things done." Take a few moments and ask them the following questions:

1. What is the best tip you could give on getting things done?
2. What is the biggest hindrance to your getting things done?

WRITE

Write a summary of what key takeaways you received from the above readings and questions you asked. Make sure your summary takeaways are written in a way that you can personalize.

CHARACTER

READ

1. "Character Counts" by Os Guinness

ASK

Think of two or three people that you have the utmost admiration for because of their character. Take a few moments and ask them the following questions:

1. What were the biggest influences in your life that helped build your character?
2. What are some examples of decisions you have made that were not easy but you knew they were the right ones?
3. What advice would you give to someone about character?

WRITE

Write a summary of what key takeaways you received from the above readings and questions you asked. Make sure your summary takeaways are written in a way that you can personalize.

TIME MANAGEMENT

READ

1. "Getting Things Done" by David Allen
2. "Time Management from the Inside Out" by Julie Morgenstern

ASK

What are your current time management tools that you use consistently?

What book on time management have you read? What were the key takeaways if you did read one?

Find someone who you view as having a very balanced life and ask them what specifically they do to achieve their balance so effectively.

WRITE

Write a summary of what key takeaways you received from the above readings and questions you asked. Make sure your summary takeaways are written in a way that you can personalize.

OPTIMISM

READ

1. "Learned Optimism" by Martin Seligman
2. "Feeling Good" by David Burns

ASK

Take a day and ask some people to point out anytime you blame, complain or criticize someone or something. This is a great self-awareness exercise. Try it for three days. Ask key people around you to truly be honest with you if they hear you blame, complain or criticize.

WRITE

Write a summary of what key takeaways you received from the above readings and questions you asked. Make sure your summary takeaways are written in a way that you can personalize.

RELATIONAL SKILLS

READ

1. "The Language of Emotional Intelligence" by Jeanne Segal

2. "The Five Dysfunctions of a Team" by Patrick Lencioni

ASK

What new relationships have you built in the past three months?

Why would people think that you are for them? Give specific examples.

Find someone who seems to be great with people. Think about three things they do really well that allows them to be so good with others.

WRITE

Write a summary of what key takeaways you received from the above readings and questions you asked. Also, how well do you do the same three things that you listed about the person above? Make sure your summary takeaways are written in a way that you can personalize.

YEARNING

READ

1. "The Goal: A Process of Ongoing Improvement" by Eliyahu Goldratt
2. "No Excuses" by Brian Tracy
3. "The Platinum Rule" by Tony Alessandra

ASK

Select three people who know you well. Ask them the following questions:

1. Do they see you as someone who takes continuous growth seriously?
2. How have they seen you grow the most over the past year?
3. What area would they love to see you grow in more?

WRITE

Write a summary of what key takeaways you received from the above readings and questions you asked. Make sure your summary takeaways are written in a way that you can personalize.

RESOURCES

RECOMMENDED READING: TOP TWENTY FAVORITES

1. **The Five Dysfunctions of a Team; Patrick Lencioni**

   A very simple and quick fable that surfaces the core issues that can break down any team. Though it's not a deep read, the truths found in this book are powerful and immediately applicable. Very few will read this book and not find immediate application in their work or personal life.

2. **The Leadership Challenge; James Kouzes & Barry Posner**

   A thoroughly researched book with findings that if taken seriously can have a profound effect on a leader's effectiveness. The five discoveries of these authors are terrific.

3. **The 7 Habits of Highly Effective People; Stephen Covey**

   Though it's been around for decades, its impact cannot be challenged. A great book to re-read every year. Can be a bit laborious to read in places but well worth the time and effort to complete it. A genuine classic.

4. **Extraordinary Relationships; Roberta Gilbert**

   One of the most thoughtful and serious books on relationships. Gilbert shows what a healthy relationship looks like and what the elements of unhealthy relationships look like. A very readable explanation of 'family systems' and how to move up the spectrum of growth.

5. **Emotional Intelligence; Daniel Goleman**

Several years old but still one of the best books on emotional intelligence today. Goleman has put EQ on the map and you would do well to read him and understand what emotional intelligence is and why it's so important to your success. An absolute classic in its field.

6. **A Failure of Nerve; Edwin Friedman**

Without a doubt one of the finest and richest books written on the topic of leadership and growth. Takes on the contemporary demand for quick fixes and immediate solutions and explains why being committed to processes more than end results is the only way to get genuine healthy results.

7. **How to Win Friends and Influence People; Dale Carnegie**

Another classic written over 75 years ago. Virtually everything Carnegie said so many years ago remains true today which is why it has been such a timeless book. Anything that is still in print after this long deserves to be read and this book is no different.

8. **Execution; Ram Charan & Larry Bossidy**

An outstanding book on the importance of strategy, processes and people, and how to execute in these critical areas. This book will be placed in the classics category in time as the content and the practical advice is incredibly relevant.

9. **In Search of Balance; Richard Swenson**

In a world where schedules are crazy and everyone seems to be consumed in busyness, Swenson's book is a welcome help to recover the necessary balance in all the important areas of life. Not a bad idea to read this book as a matter of discipline each year to make sure you are not falling off the rails.

10. **Humilitas; John Dickson**

Dickson talks about a not very talked about topic these days, but he shows how important humility is in every area of our life in order to truly experience success and satisfaction. A simple yet profound book in many respects. The do-it-yourself cowboy mentality these days will be challenged greatly by the message of this book.

11. **Change Your Thinking Change Your Life; Brian Tracy**

It's been said that life happens between the ears and Tracy shows just how true that is. Our attitudes and beliefs construct most of what life looks like for us so learning to control what you think will in fact change how you view most of your life.

12. **Organizing From the Inside Out; Julie Morgenstern**

You would never think an author could present over 300 pages on organizing your life and work effectively, but Morgenstern sure does. If organization is an issue for you, then this book will have many gems for you to consider.

13. **Boundaries for Leaders; Dr. Henry Cloud**

One of the great challenges of any leader is learning to

balance and protect his time. It's very easy to allow the demands of people all around you to cause you to take on things that are not yours to take on. More than that, as leaders, it's critical to not feel the responsibility of other people's struggles and failures. Cloud shows you how to maintain healthy boundaries as a leader so that you are as effective as possible.

14. **Cultivating the Strategic Mind; Dr. Blake Leath**

    A true gem of a book on what it means to be strategic. Leath writes in a style that is a pure joy to experience and his discussion includes multiple levels of how to be a more effective strategic thinker. Great writing and a great model make for a truly great book.

15. **The Narcissism Epidemic; Jean Twenge & Keith Campbell**

    An excellent treatment of the rise of a self-absorbed culture. You cannot read this book without looking inward and asking yourself if you take on any of the characteristics of narcissism that exist all around us. Great leadership is about serving others. So read this and challenge yourself to be exactly the opposite of what the authors describe.

16. **No Excuses; Brian Tracy**

    In a day where blaming others seems so natural, Tracy argues that the only person there is to blame in life is yourself. Blaming others does you no good, but taking full responsibility empowers you to achieve virtually anything you set your mind to. An easy-to-read and inspiring book to take ownership of your life and go after whatever it is that you want.

17. **Conversationally Speaking; Alan Garner**

    It seems that the art of good conversation is slowly dying in our culture. Alan Garner comes to the rescue by showing all of the elements of effective communication and what the mechanics are of an effective conversation. Read this and put what he says into practice and I will promise you that your conversations with people will go to an entirely new level.

18. **If Aristotle Ran General Motors; Tom Morris**

    As a former professional philosopher, Morris takes on the business world by introducing some of the most important virtues of mankind to corporate America. Truth, beauty, goodness and unity are powerful and timeless concepts that if taken seriously will help catapult any organization closer to achieving its long term goals.

19. **How To Influence People; John Maxwell**

    A very short yet very poignant book that deals exactly with what it takes to be a greater influence with the people around you. Maxwell is a master of simplicity. He knows how to make things practical so that you can begin putting them into practice right away. If you want greater influence in your life, then this book will be a great benefit to you. It won't take long to read, but it will provide a lifetime of benefit.

20. **The 12 Bad Habits That Hold Good People Back; James Waldroop & Timothy Butler**

    Some people never get to where they want to go because they have certain patterns of behavior that hinder them from further progress. What is tragic is that often times they are unaware of what those behaviors are. Waldroop and Butler do an excellent job of identifying 12 of these behaviors and what you can do about them. It's not always what you do that will cause your success. Sometimes it's what you don't do!

SOURCES, CITATIONS & NOTES

Preface

- "The Sundial" by Henry Van Dyke is found on a sundial at Wells College.

Introduction

- The reason I chose the word "VICTORY" for my acronym is because victory is the one thing everyone ultimately wants in every important area of life. Life can be very hard. Marriage often has seasons of great challenges. Parenting can be incredibly challenging. Athletic or artistic excellence requires significant challenges and struggles, and leading a successful organization is often filled with never-ending obstacles. For these reasons we all strive for victory.

Chapter One: The Necessity of Vision

- Arthur Schopenhauer was an influential German philosopher known for his pessimism. One of his most famous lines was "The world is my representation," hence his quote found in this chapter.
- *Blogs.hbr.org/2007/10/the-importance-of-vision/*
- Proverbs 29:18 (The theological context for this wisdom saying is a prophetic revelation from God. In other words, the text is saying that mankind needs God's revelation. The principle is also true that vision is necessary for success in any endeavor.)
- Each famous person listed has an incredible story of how vision transformed their lives and has led to the inspiration of millions. A great exercise would be to Google each person and read a short bio of what their vision was and how it impacted their lives.

- *http://www.huffingtonpost.com/2013/05/26/oldest-to-climb-mount-everest-yuichiro-miura_n_3339911.html*
- *http://everything2.com/title/Chevreul%2527s+pendulum*

Chapter Two: The Power of Initiative

- "No problem is problem" is one of the great quotes used by one of the great standard bearers of quality, Toyota Motor Corporation. The main idea is that we should always be looking for ways to take action and improve things. Excellence does not come from sitting back and waiting for things to improve. We must make them happen.

  www.leanblog.org/2010/05/no-problems-is-problem-video
- Bob Rotella, in his excellent book "Golf is Not a Game of Perfect," talks about the role that the balance beam plays in helping athletes understand how fear can significantly impede their performance.
- *http://www.biography.com/people/madam-cj-walker-9522174*

Chapter Three: Your Character: Who Are You?

- "The tongue in your mouth and the tongue in your shoe should point in the same direction" is a great picture of what a person of integrity looks like. What we say (tongue in our mouth) and what we do (our actions) should be consistent if we are going to be considered people of integrity.
- *http://www.huffingtonpost.com/2014/05/27/runner-falls-wins-race-heather-dorniden_n_5395232.html*
- (Brown-Driver-Briggs Hebrew Lexicon) shows how often the Hebrew word translated as "character" in English means strength, mighty, army, etc…

  http://biblehub.com/bdb/2428.htm

- Stephen Covey's book "The 7 Habits of Highly Effective People" is sensational. I've read it several times over the years and have found each habit to be spot on. However the habit of "Seeking First to Understand Before You Seek to be Understood" has been one of the most practical and effective tools I have applied in my own life.

Chapter Four: Time Management: Do You Know Your Spending Habits?

- "Lack of direction, not lack of time, is the problem. We all have 24 hours!" This quote gets right to the heart of the time management. Time management is all about being clear on what "direction" you want to go, which ONLY comes from having a clear vision of what you want.
- Andy Stanley is the one who said "Most people don't lead their lives, they accept their lives." This idea is expressed well in his book "The Principle of the Path." Essentially the idea is that all choices exist on a path and all paths lead to a destination. So we need to be intentional about what choices we make because they all set us on a path to a certain destination.
- *http://www.nytimes.com/2014/07/15/sports/golf/british-open-2014-john-singleton-lives-his-fantasy-as-golfs-walter-mitty.html*
- A more recent study on the importance of writing down your goals can be found at:

  http://www.dominican.edu/dominicannews/study-backs-up-strategies-for-achieving-goals

Chapter Five: Optimism: What Does Your Tomorrow Look Like?

- *http://www.huffingtonpost.com/karl-a-pillemer-phd/how-to-stop-worrying-reduce-stress_b_2989589.html*

- Viktor Frankl's life experience and wisdom are quite inspiring. Go to YouTube.com and type in "Interview with Dr. Frankl Part 1" and watch him communicate the essential tenets of how to endure and overcome enormous struggle in life.
- One of the most uplifting and challenging people I have ever heard is Nick Vujicic. Check out his website *www.lifewithoutlimbs.org* and watch his videos. Be warned: prepare to see most of your own struggles in a different perspective.
- What makes us different from all the rest of animal creation is that we have the power of choice. We get to decide how we want things to look in our minds. We should never forfeit this gift of choice that we have at every moment of our lives.

Chapter Six: Relational Skills: The Building Blocks of Life

- For a more thorough study of John D. Rockefeller's life, read the excellent biography entitled "Titan: The Life of John D. Rockefeller" by Ron Chernow.
- For a good overview article on the relationship between academic success and life success, read the following article by Keld Jensen:

  http://www.forbes.com/sites/keldjensen/2012/04/12/intelligence-is-overrated-what-you-really-need-to-succeed/
- Daniel Goleman has also done extensive research in this field of emotional competencies vs. technical competencies and success. Read the following article by Goleman:

  http://qz.com/87154/emotional-intelligence-is-a-better-predictor-of-success-than-iq/
- One of the best books on the market today on how to have great conversations is "Conversationally Speaking" by Alan Garner. There are few skills as beneficial as being able to create,

drive and sustain conversations with anyone you talk to. This is indeed a dying art today.

Chapter Seven: Yearning: You Never Arrive Until It's Over

- "Improvement begins with 'I' " is one of my favorite quotes. Its meaning is quite obvious. No one can do it for you. We can make excuses and give reasons for not doing things until we are blue in the face, but the bottom line is that nothing changes. Improvement begins with YOU.
- The Nola Ochs story is an inspirational example that life should be a constant pursuit of improving ourselves.

  http://www.huffingtonpost.com/2010/05/12/nola-ochs-98-years-old-to_n_573670.html;
- "In order to discover new lands, one must consent to lose site of the shore for a long time." Without question, this is my favorite quote. All of us long for new lands along with all the benefits that come with those new experiences. However, the price of finding the new lands is giving up the comforts of today.
- In Malcolm Gladwell's book "Outliers," he talks about the now famous 10,000 hours rule. In order to be considered an expert at anything, it will require about 10,000 hours of focused practice. Whether or not that research stands or will be adjusted by future research, the principle is true that excellence comes from consistent practice and focus.

WALTER NUSBAUM

Walter Nusbaum is CEO of The Nusbaum Group. As an accomplished speaker, coach and organizational consultant, Walter has spoken to and worked with thousands of successful leaders and knows exactly what it takes to achieve great results. He has spent over 20 years training and developing executives, business people, athletes and leaders of non-profit organizations. He has worked individually and corporately with executives from a broad spectrum of organizations such as the HollyFrontier Corporation, Williams Financial Group, Sandia National Laboratories, Buckeye Partners, Lockheed Martin and many others.

As a growth strategist, Walter focuses on helping organizations develop their human capital, from the executive level to the front-line employee, in order to help them successfully achieve their objectives.

Through his life and executive coaching practice, he has taught, mentored and coached hundreds of leaders on topics such as growing trust, developing effective communication skills and driving a performance based culture.

He earned a B.A. in Strategic Management from the University of North Texas in Denton, Texas and an M.A. in Religious Studies from Dallas Theological Seminary. Walter and his wife, Stacey, live outside of Dallas in Denton, Texas with their four children.

Made in the USA
Columbia, SC
12 September 2017